Wings in the Wind:

The Armistice Day

Storm of 1940

JON STEFFES

ISBN: 0985856904

ISBN-13: 9780985856908

DEDICATION

This book is dedicated to my father, Robert Nic Steffes. I miss him every day, more so when I am hunting and fishing, following in his footsteps.

A dedication is also made to the many hunters who perished during the Armistice Day Storm of 1940, and to Max Conrad and others who helped save lives.

Bob Steffes, while in the U.S. Navy in 1943.

ACKNOWLEDGMENTS

Thank you Michael Sieve for allowing me to use your wonderful painting as my cover. His painting captured the vision that I had for my cover. Mr. Sieve's work is available through Wild Wings. **See more of his work on** http://www.wildwings.com/

A big thank you to Jarrod and Kathy Nelson, my excellent editors. I appreciate all your hard work and encouragement on this journey.

CHAPTER 1

***

The battered old canoe slid smoothly through the water, occasionally creasing its way past the stiff, green stalks of wild rice. A pair of mallards erupted into flight just ahead as the canoe rounded the corner into a dead end bay, only 60 or 70 yards in diameter. Duke, a black lab just over a year old, stood tensely at the helm, his feet on the bow, watching the ducks.

Bob Steffes paused his stroke, resting his paddle on the frame of the old wooden canoe momentarily to watch the ducks, "Stay Duke," Bob said with a chuckle.

Duke peered back at Bob, waiting for the blast

of a shotgun.

"Sorry Pal, can't shoot 'em for a couple months," Bob told his dog with a smile.

Kicking up ducks in a canoe was not an uncommon event for Bob and Duke. At 16 years of age, Bob had already logged many hours in his canoe, exploring the back waters of the Mississippi, fishing and duck hunting. The bay they had just entered was, as he liked to say, "his spot". Getting to his spot took a little work. It was a two hour canoe trip one way, and Bob had made the trip many times before. He had put in at Vercota Landing just south of Prairie Island and north of the Spillway that connected Minnesota and Wisconsin.

The year was 1940, and the upper Mississippi River system of lock and dams were less than 10 years old. The Minnesota side of the Mississippi River had the spillway, a concrete dike that allowed the water to gently drop to the next level, allowing for the eight foot depth the Corp of Engineers required at this upper stage of the Mississippi. The lock and dams were either on the Wisconsin or Minnesota side and controlled the level of water elevation, allowing barge and pleasure boats to navigate the drop. The opposite side usually consisted of the backwaters and spillways. On the Wisconsin side, Lock and Dam #5A hugged the shore of Fountain City just downriver. Up river, Lock and Dam #5 was on the Minnesota side. Nearly ten miles of backwaters were Bob's to explore, hunt, and fish.

After putting in at Vercota, Bob paddled Crooked Slough until it merged with Pickerel Run, fast flowing as it drained the valley just upstream of Minnesota City, Minnesota. Several miles of paddling on Pickerel Run, Bob took a left into Twin Lakes, just before Pickerel Run emptied into the Mississippi River. It was a mile across Twin Lakes, mostly a shallow, weedy lake, to the other side, where, tucked along the shore line, Bob had found an entrance to another slough, unnamed and only 100 yards long. It was at the mouth of this 100 yard long slough that Bob claimed as his spot. Surprisingly, the slough was deep, 14 feet, scoured out by the spring floods, pushing water out of the many valleys in southern Minnesota, rushing toward the Mississippi River, having to fight its way through the maze of sloughs and channels. But as the slough entered the bay, the depth rose to a sandy shelf eight feet below the water's surface. It's this shelf that Bob fished now, letting his canoe drift in the light breeze in the mouth of the bay. He jigged with a white, three-eighth ounce lead jig head, tipped with a fat head minnow, bouncing his rod tip ever so slightly, trying to entice a walleye.

It didn't take long before the rapid tapping at the end of his line told Bob to lower his rod tip for only about a half second before quickly pulling up, setting the hook into the fish below. The battle was quick. Bob let the fish fight only briefly, before sliding it along the canoe where he pulled it aboard without his net. A walleye, only about 12 inches long. The hard toothy mouth of the little fish meant an easy release, the hook not buried too deeply. Bob admired the small fish for the couple seconds it took to get its bearings upon its release into the water; the sun catching the golden flecks in its scales before it darted down into the muddy depths. Bob hooked on a fresh minnow, guiding the hook through the minnow's lower lip and coming out its upper, then dropped it back in the water with a plop. Eight feet of line let out, and he felt bottom. One turn of the reel and he was off bottom and back to fishing. He just had enough time to run his paddle in the water, one-handed, to straighten his canoe, perpendicular to the wind, when he had to again set the hook. A little bigger fight this time; the walleye forced Bob to lean forward and allow the fish to circle the front of the canoe and tire before coming to the surface and finding its way into the net. A plump 17 inch walleye swam into Bob's net, a good eater. This one went into the wire basket tied to the support of his seat before dropping his line in again.

Bob could only spare an hour of fishing today, or he'd have to double time it back to the landing. Luckily it only took 45 minutes to have four nice fish in the basket and start heading for home. The wind would be on his back on the way across Twin Lakes and his arms were fresh, Bob went for his record. Every time he made the one mile trek across the lake, he timed himself. Just a hair over 13 minutes was his record. He felt good today, and he felt his odds were good to get under 13. As he exited the slough, he checked his watch and started off. He resisted the urge to dig his paddle too deep as he gathered speed. Instead, he concentrated on short, quick strokes.

Twin Lakes was not really a lake, rather one of many shallow watersheds, between the main channel of the Mississippi River and the Minnesota Bluffs. At this portion of the waterway, the main channel ran tight to the Wisconsin Bluffs, where quaint little river towns such as Fountain City and Alma sat, perched on the narrow strip of flat land along the river, or nestled on the hill sides. The main channel was not too far away, just on the other side of a row of wooded islands to Bob's left, less than a mile now across Twin Lakes. The thousands of islands throughout the bottoms between the main channel and the Minnesota bluffs came in all sizes. However, most of the them were nothing more than narrow pieces of land running parallel to the flow of the river, broken in their chains by various channels and sloughs; a maze of water only ventured by those who knew their way around.

Bob felt his chances were good to beat his record. He just had to get to the mouth of Pickerel Run before stopping his individual race. The wind was good, but occasional gusts kept pushing the nose of his canoe to the right, and he had to correct his course more often than he liked. As he cruised closer to the mouth of the creek, he spied the big dead elm that marked his finish line, jutting out from the narrow point of land that separated the lake from the creek. Only 50 yards to go and he would pass within casting distance from the tree. He strained hard, breathing rapidly, trying to pour it on at the finish. Passing the old tree, he quickly checked his watch…13 minutes and 50 seconds. The wind had done him in again. Too much of a north wind usually messed up his race. Wind from the northwest was the best. That gave him a direct shot across the lake, where he didn't have to fight to keep the nose of his canoe straight.

He knew he shouldn't be goofing around with tearing across the lake anyway. He had a big baseball game tonight and should really be conserving his energy for the game. This was Bob's first year playing on the Winona town summer baseball team. He was a pitcher, a good one according to the other players in town, and he didn't want to screw things up by not being on top of his game. His team was a perfect 8 and 0, and he hoped to keep it that way.

Graham and McGuires was the local sporting goods store in downtown Winona that sponsored Bob's team. His team consisted of juniors, seniors, and recent Winona High School graduates.

He could take his time now on Pickerel Run, then on Crooked Slough. He was going downstream now and by making a turn to the south, the wind was now on his back. Checking his watch he saw that it was just past 2:00, plenty of time to get back to Vercoda Landing and then home. His game was at 6:00, but the guys would be expecting him at 5:00 to warm up before taking the field.

He cruised along steadily, glad to be able to get a day off of work on a Friday. Of course, working for his dad at Nic's Auto during the summer didn't pay him much, but it gave him the opportunity to get out fishing or hunting from time to time. His dad, Nic, understood. A sportsman himself, he was guilty of sneaking off to enjoy what the river valley had to offer. Like Bob, his weakness was duck hunting. Deer and pheasants were great, and they added to the meals in the freezer too, but duck hunting in Winona was king. The Mississippi flyway offered a variety of birds: mallards, wigeons, canvasbacks, wood ducks, shovelers - a little bit of everything came through when the winter weather pushed them south. Nearly everybody in town had a reliable boat in the garage and a weather-hardy dog in the kennel.

It was 4:20 when Bob made it back to the boat landing. It just took a moment or two for him to load his canoe atop his father's '36 Ford pickup and head for home. A quick bite to eat and he'd be ready for the game at 6:00.

CHAPTER 2

***

Bob pulled his dad's truck into the driveway his family shared with their neighbors, Sonny and Joyce Ehlers. He drove to the back of their big white home and parked the truck in front of the one stall garage. Duke leapt out as soon as Bob opened the truck's door and scrambled about the back yard, sniffing about as if checking to see if anyone entered his domain since he had been gone. Bob hoisted the canoe from the bed of the pickup, and holding onto the side rails, jerked it over his head and marched toward the three car garage next to the neighboring home where two posts were pounded into the ground. Bob carefully lowered the canoe onto the two by fours running parallel to the ground attached to the four by four posts in the ground.

Bob's father, Nic, owned the six unit, three story apartment house next door along with the garage Bob now stood next to. Bob, along with his 21 year old brother Charles, nicknamed Buzz because of his affinity for flat top haircuts, and his 14 year old sister Esther, helped their parents take care of the old apartment house. There was always some work to be done on the building. Railings needed painting, holes in the roof to patch, as well as electrical work. In the summer, everyone pitched in with mowing the lawn for two homes. The winter was really taxing when snow needed to be shoveled from not only the Steffes's long driveway, but the three car driveway in front of the large apartment garage.

The benefits of helping his father run the apartment building were there however. He had access to a garage stall that he hoped to one day pull his own truck into. The stall had enough room in front to hang his waders and decoy bag from the rafters. In the winter he could also hang his canoe. For now, the canoe would stay outside. He'd be using it throughout the summer and then into fall during duck season. Nic was an outdoorsman like his sons, and had even rigged rollers under the crawl space of the apartment building's front porch so they could slide the old 14 foot aluminum boot under the crawl space of the house. Even young Bob could easily slide the boat off the trailer and push it, on the rollers, under the porch. His dad let him park the trailer in the alley behind his garage.

The little table in the corner of the garage was used for fish cleaning and deboning the deer he shot in the winter. In only a couple minutes, he filleted out the walleyes and rinsed the meat off with the hose in the yard. Taking the fresh fillets in hand, he whistled for Duke, closed his lab in his kennel, and jogged up the three steps into the back door of his home into his family's kitchen.

His mom, Ellen Steffes, was in the kitchen, getting dinner ready. The smell of her famous meatloaf filled the home. But Bob's dinner was a ham sandwich sitting on a plate on the kitchen table. She knew Bob would always fish as long as he could, thus allowing him little time to eat a meal, even her meatloaf, baked potatoes, and fresh asparagus. She had tried to make him sit down and eat for years, but the boy had such passion for his outdoor adventures, that he rarely made time to sit for a good meal.

"A quick sandwich, Mom, and I need to get to my game," Bob said to his smiling mother.

"Think we can stay unbeaten?" He asked his mom as he ate, standing in the kitchen, pouring a glass of milk. As always, she just shrugged, smiled, and continued washing her asparagus.

Content with a shrug, Bob hustled up the stairs to his second floor bedroom and began getting on his baseball uniform, all while eating a sandwich.

The Steffes house was like many in the central part of Winona, about 1700 square feet, square in shape, with two floors and a basement. The main level consisted of a kitchen, a living room, a bathroom, and a big dining room. Bob's bedroom was upstairs, along with three other bedrooms, and a full bathroom. His bedroom was once a second story porch, but his father had enclosed it shortly after Bob was born. It was small, only about six by nine feet, but it had just enough room for a small closet, a bed, and a narrow dresser that took up one whole wall.

Besides, most of Bob's possessions were in the basement. The Steffes basement was a litany of hunting and fishing items. Although half the basement was finished, containing a couch and a handmade bar for when his father was entertaining his hunting buddies, the rest of the basement was a jungle of waders, decoy bags, hunting coats, and fishing poles, hung or latched to the rafters. Metal cabinets housed the guns and ammo. Wooden boxes sat on shelves, full of assorted hats and gloves. A variety of boots sat on wooden planks attached to the bare studs of the walls.

Bob took just a moment to place his fishing rod and tackle box in the corner with over a dozen other rods, threw on his baseball uniform, set out for him on the washing machine by this mother, before grabbing his baseball mitt and racing up the basement stairs and out the door.

"See ya Mom!" Bob shouted and jumped back into his father's truck and headed to the ball field.

CHAPTER 3

***

His team was already warming up by the time he got to the ball field. Another game was going on and teams used the area between two fields to warm up. Bob jumped in with Al, his catcher, and began to warm up his arm by throwing. A few minutes of easy tosses and he would start pitching.

"How were they biting?" Al asked as he and Bob were beginning to throw.

"Not bad," Bob said as he gradually increased his velocity. "Kept four to fillet."

"Beat your record across Twin Lakes?" Al smiled, knowing his pitcher couldn't resist a challenge to compete, even if it was in a canoe, and it was against himself.

"I was off by less than a minute," Bob said

with a shrug. "Next time."

Bob found that he liked playing for the town team in the summer even better than playing high school ball. As a sophomore this past spring, he was a young guy trying to earn a starting spot somewhere. He tried pitching the year before as a freshman, and found that he had a knack for it. He always had a strong arm, able to fire a fastball in the low 80's. But, with some practice, he had developed a change-up that could baffle the opposing batter. He would fire a couple heaters across the plate, and then come in with a change-up that would seemingly coast in at barely 60 miles per hour. This big change of speeds would get the batter way out in front of the pitch, often leading to a weak groundball out. But his favorite pitch was his screwball. It was like his fastball, but he was able to roll the ball off his ring and little finger just slightly enough to make the ball tail into the batter. This was his strike out pitch. He had found that when he had a batter down two strikes, he could recognize when a determined batter would dig in to protect the plate. He could almost guess when the batter was going to swing, trying not to go down looking at a called third strike. That's when he'd bring his screwball. The ball would start out high in the zone, right in the batter's line of sight, and tail in to the batter, jamming him high and tight out of the strike zone, with too much velocity to catch up with. Many a frustrated batter had cussed out Bob after striking out throughout the past two seasons.

When his teammates saw the teams on the other field line up to shake hands, Bob and his team began walking along the foul line fence toward their dugout. The bleachers were full. The top divisions were always scheduled on Friday nights. His McGuires team was a force, winning the City Championship two out of the last three years. And, in the last six years, the championship went to either McGuires or Wojeski Stone from Minnesota City. Wojeskis won it in 1934, 35, and 36. McGuires won it in 37 and 38, and last year Wojeskis took back the title.

Last year was a real battle. Bob was in the bleachers watching as it went down to the wire. He watched his high school teammate, Ed Wojeski give up only four hits while Ted Spencer gave up only three for McGuires. But, Ed was not only a formidable pitcher he was also a superb hitter. His home run in the bottom of the last inning won it for Wojeski Stone.

Ed's father owned Wojeski Stone Quarry, a thriving business producing some of the best granite in the Midwest, and had been sponsoring the team from Minnesota City, just up river from Winona, for nearly ten years now. Bob was high school teammates with Ed, a recently graduated senior, but this summer they were opponents, as Bob played for the Winona town team.

Ed was two years older than Bob. In the spring, with Ed a senior and Bob a sophomore, the competitiveness of both teens was obvious. Ed was the star pitcher and wanted to keep that status. When Ed wasn't pitching, he played third base, Bob's other position. Ed graduated from Winona High and starred in football, basketball, and baseball. Ed had opted not to go to college, choosing instead to work for his father. Winona stone was of great quality. The granite pulled from the quarry was in high demand and the Wojeski family was quickly becoming the wealthiest in town, if not in Southeastern Minnesota. Ed and Bob were a lot alike. Both were competitive, focused on the sport of baseball, and avid outdoorsman. However, Ed was huge - a mammoth of a man, six foot three and well over 200 pounds, an imposing lineman in football, and a danger in the lane in basketball. Bob was only five-foot-nine. His stocky build helped him push the scales to 190. He was eager for the chance to be the star pitcher on the McGuires Winona town baseball team, out from underneath the shadow of Ed, as the upperclassman. As soon as summer started, Bob started working out at the YMCA every morning, lifting weights. He started canoeing to his fishing spots instead of taking his boat. His goal was to become stronger and leaner, all with the goal of leading his team against Minnesota City's Wojeski Stone team.

McGuires was the home team. His teammates, his buddies, took the field. Their opponent, The Winona Sportsman's Club, prepared in their dugout to bat first. Most of the guys on his McGuires team this year were guys in their late teens or early twenties. He knew some of them pretty well, having watched a lot of baseball games each summer, playing high school baseball with them, or spending time in the river bottoms with them hunting or fishing.

Al, his catcher, was one of his best friends, a reliable hunting buddy, and only one of three guys on the team that was 16 years old. Al had been working for his dad while going to high school since he was 14, doing masonry work in town. At only age 16, Al was already an exceptional mason, working alongside his father building chimneys mostly. He already had his career laid out as a mason. Hauling brick after school and in the summers made him a solid, immovable presence behind the plate. Base runners in their division knew that if there was a close play at the plate, they had better slide. Trying to take out Al was going to be a losing proposition for them. His other main hunting buddy was Cliff, his shortstop.

Cliff was the other guy his age on the team. Cliff was the one who visited the mound whenever Bob got into a jam. His focused, calming presence was always appreciated, whether on the baseball diamond, or in the duck blind. All the guys on McGuires tried to contribute to one of the best summer league baseball teams in the area. Jobs, families, and other responsibilities sometimes got in the way, but they had managed to keep the team intact. Bob hoped to be a dependable teammate for many years to come.

The game went by fast. McGuires dominated. Bob was at the top of his game, striking out 13 and giving up only five hits. Two opposing runners were even gutsy enough to run on Tom Baab, playing left field and with a cannon for an arm. He threw them both out, his throw beating the runners to the plate by several steps. McGuires was now 9-0. Bob and his teammates shook hands with their opponents, an older group of guys who had been in the league for a long time, once being a powerhouse just like McGuires. Smiles and pats on the back were all around. The guys from The Sportsman's Club had accepted that they were no longer an elite team. They just loved getting out and playing, and it showed, their wives and children in the bleachers cheering their effort.

McGuires began leaving the field together, "Umph!" Bob was bumped into as slipped through the fence next to the backstop. He stopped, momentarily off balance, and realized he was face to face with Ed Wojeski.

Ed stopped as well, looking down at the smaller and younger pitcher, a slight nod, but no apology.

CHAPTER 4

***

After the game against The Sportsman's Club, Bob sat in the bleachers with Cliff and Al and watched Wojeski's play. Most of his teammates stuck around, scattered amongst the other people watching the action. Cold Fountain City Brew, beer brewed right across the river, was distributed from a cooler and consumed by the older guys on his team, and the young men of McGuires sat back and watched their opponents for next week's game dismantle Peerless Chain.

The evening began to cool, a refreshing relief from the heat of the game he had just played and his afternoon canoe trip. Bob relished these evenings, sitting with his friends in the bleachers.

The older guys were sipping cold beer, being old enough to drink, while Bob, Al, and Cliff drank soda. If his dad, Nic, ever caught him drinking alcohol, there would be hell to pay, so he always resisted temptation, and stuck to his Coca-Cola. The evening was cool and they were watching baseball, these were the days Bob loved.

Bob always felt the tension of what his future would hold. Military, college, getting a job, he didn't know. It bothered him that he was so uncertain what was ahead of him. But on nights like tonight, those things didn't weigh on him.

Bob wasn't as well-off as some of his friends. Some of the older guys he played ball with already had fancy cars or their own house. He had baseball. And he was good at it. He had to keep reminding himself that he was living a good life. Aside from going to school and working with his father to earn a little extra spending money, he could hunt and fish in the fall, ice fish and trap in the winter, park his boat below the lock and dams in the spring to catch his limit of walleyes, and in the summer, he could play baseball on the weekends. He had nearly everything he wanted. He looked down the row of bleachers to a cheering brunette in a white dress, with a white bow in her hair to match her dress. He didn't have Marie. When he was fishing with Duke he thought of Marie. When he was working on a car in his dad's garage, he thought of Marie. He spent his whole sophomore year, sitting in class, thinking of Marie. It was hard for his mind to escape from her, especially on the weekends. Every Friday night, she was there, in the bleachers, watching the games. Sometimes he wondered how he could pitch, staring at his catcher, getting his signs, when she was there, just in the corner of his eye. When he came to bat, he wondered if she was watching him.

The game was ending now with another Ed Wojeski pitch, fanning a batter. Wojeskis had won again. Undefeated and forcing the final game of the season next week against Graham and McGuires. Wojeskis finished shaking hands and filtered out of the dugout. Bob watched as Ed was greeted with a hug and a kiss from Marie.

Sometimes Bob thought Ed was the one who had it all. A good paying job, a beautiful girlfriend, and a city baseball title to defend.

For now, he just needed to concentrate on finishing high school. Maybe after college he'd work for his dad for a while at Nic's Garage, fixing cars, and his dad's other area of expertise, fixing bicycles. But, his dad, Nic, showed no signs of giving it all up just yet. Nic was an excellent mechanic, but still had plenty of years left wielding a wrench. His father knew that his youngest son would not end up following in his footsteps as a mechanic. Yet that wasn't stopping Nic from putting some pressure on his 16 year old to have a plan for after high school. Nic Steffes always had a plan. He knew what day of the month he would make purchases for his garage. He knew that in two years he was going to buy another apartment house in town to bring in more money. He knew that every five years he goes to Ontario with a couple friends for bear hunting and walleye fishing. He also knew that his 21 year old son, Buzz, Bob's older brother, would be the one to take over the garage when Nic hit age 62. Buzz had this in his plans as well. But it drove Nic crazy that his 16 year old son had no idea what he wanted to do after high school.

Bob had a few ideas though. Barges were becoming more and more common on the river. The lock and dam system had created a big demand for workers to join Avondale Industries, a barge and maritime company expanding their business up the river. Workers were getting good money. Bob nearly applied to work that summer on the barges, to see if that was the direction he wanted to go. However summers were long on the barge, and if that would become his career, the job would have had him on the river from ice out in April, to first ice in November. That would pretty much put an end to his summer fishing and duck hunting. Then he might as well go to college. He also had some ideas to either take some test to become a mail carrier, or join the military after graduation. The Germans had begun the Battle of Britain, and he figured it was only a matter of time before Roosevelt jumped in. Bob craved excitement, but also wanted what he had had earlier in the day, just him and Duke in a canoe catching walleyes.

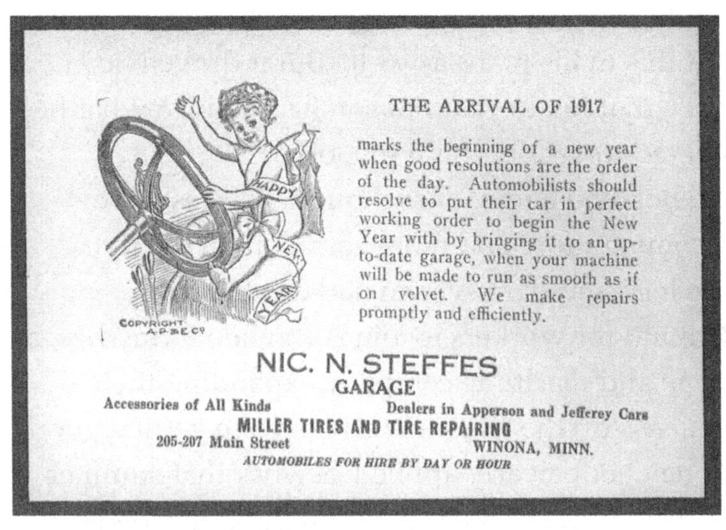

CHAPTER 5

***

When Bob pulled up at his father's garage the next morning, he tried to dive right into his work. His father always considered Saturday to be his busiest day.

"People don't want to disrupt their lives and their jobs to get their cars or bikes fixed," his father would always say. Everybody knew Nic Steffes would get to the garage early Saturday morning, and stay until everybody had their repairs completed. If the work didn't get done Saturday, he knew Sunday was going to be another work day. Ever since early on in high school Bob knew his father would be depending upon him to be there on Saturdays to help him. Besides the pay, his motivation to get things done on a Saturday afternoon at his father's garage was knowing that if he got done, he would have time to go out with his friends. Hard work and long hours was an expectation his father had and it was not a choice for Bob. He needed to follow his father's beliefs.

Besides, he knew he wasn't going to be a mechanic all his life. He wasn't the only son of Nic Steffes working at the garage. Bob's brother, Charles, 21 and five years older, was becoming as much of a mechanic as his father. Buzz was all about cars. He could care less about hunting, fishing, or sports, or even other guys' girlfriends for that matter. He loved to fix things. Buzz never was a good athlete. In high school, he had started having some breathing problems, which got worse soon after graduation. He had to learn to live with it, taking his time with things, never trying to exert himself. This just added to his desire to be a great mechanic. If he couldn't be a star athlete or paddle a canoe across a lake in record time like his younger brother, he would become an expert at fixing cars.

With Buzz and his father carrying the load with the car repairs, Bob's job was to do the simpler tasks in the garage and act as the delivery person. His father thought that superior customer service would always gain him more future business. So, one of Bob's main jobs consisted of cramming his bike in the back of a repaired car and driving it to the customer's home. From there, he would bike back to the garage. If his bike wouldn't fit in the vehicle, he would jog back. With three mechanics working on the weekend and great customer service, Nic's Garage flourished.

By three o'clock, the heat of mid-August had invaded the garage. Bob had just pedaled into the garage bay, having just gotten back from delivering Mr. Thompson's 32' Ford. Al was waiting for him, leaning against a car. Next to him, Buzz leaned in under the hood.

Buzz, without even looking up, yelled out, "Bob, get over here and lend me a hand!"

Al just smirked, sipping on a bottle of soda.

Buzz seemed in a hurry, which was good. Sometimes going out with friends on a Saturday night was held up because Buzz, not having any plans, would take his own sweet time. He must have a poker game planned with his friends tonight Bob figured.

"What do you think?" Al asked once Buzz

released Bob from his task under the hood of the car. "You think you can get outta here by 7 or 8? We can hit the wing dam over by the chimney.

"I think Buzz is hustling today. Should be able to finish up by seven at the latest," Bob whispered with a confident nod. "Can you grab my rod and reel on the way over?"

"Will do. I'll pick you up at 7:00," Al said, chugging the last of his soda and putting it on a workbench on his way out of the garage.

The chimney was where those Bob's age went in the evening. The chimney was really just the remains of an old chimney, what was left from an old house along the east channel, a secondary channel just off the main flow of the Mississippi River. The old remains of the chimney were now used as a fire pit. Bob and his buddies such as Al and Tom weren't legal drinking age like some of the guys on his town baseball team, unable to go to bars such as the Riverboat Tavern or even Swedes Bar, which were popular hang outs of his older teammates. So, they had found their own place to hang out.

But, just through the woods beyond the chimney was a wing dam, a line of rocks underwater, set in place to slow the current coming off the main channel of the Mississippi

River entering the east channel. That was where Al and Bob were heading tonight. In August, the smallmouth bass were firing up and sitting below the wing dams, waiting for baitfish to come over the top of the underwater line of rocks, an easy meal for a predator fish like the smallmouth.

At 7:00, Bob was vigorously washing the grease and oil off his hands in the big metal sink in the corner of his father's garage when Al walked in.

"Let's go!" Al chirped, a devilish smile on his face. "Times a wastin'!"

"Hold your horses!" Bob replied, drying his hands on the big towel hanging on the wall.

Bob stripped off his shirt and reached into his locker along the wall for a fresh one, as Al tossed him a paper bag.

"Knew you'd be hungry!" Al said and headed out the open garage door.

"Did you make it or did your mom?" Bob shouted behind him with a laugh.

"Does it matter?" Al yelled back, climbing into his car.

Bob shrugged and took a bite, "Pop, I'm taking off, be back home later!" he yelled to his father, shuffling through papers in his little office.

"Yep!" was Nic's reply.

Bob knew his father trusted him. He worked hard. He tried to get through high school with good grades. He even avoided hanging out in bars with some of his baseball teammates.

The young men drove through downtown Winona and turned right onto Main Street and began the climb over the Mississippi High Bridge stretching over the main channel of the Mississippi. After a couple hundred yards the bridge deck began its decent onto Latsch Island where the marina was to the left and the bathhouse, beach, and 40 foot slide kept people entertained in the hot summers- swimming and relaxing on the sandy beach.

Bob and Al went to the right and swung past the many cars lining the road in front of the bathhouse, consisting of locker rooms, a restroom, and a concession stand for the patrons using the beach. Even during the evening, the heat of August kept a great many swimmers at the beach, taking advantage of the remaining hour or so of daylight.

Al swung his car to the left and drove across the wagon bridge, a much smaller bridge that stretched across the east channel, crossing into Wisconsin on the other side. The road was a dead end, with just a few boat houses tucked in just off the road, sitting on the backwater sloughs. Across the wagon bridge, a dirt road turned to the right, running parallel to the east channel through the woods. A half mile of rutted, dusty road later, they came to a dead end in the road, opening up to an area just big enough to do a u-turn with a car. Right in the middle was the remains of an old chimney, crumbled, and only three feet off the ground.

Al pulled his car to the side, pulling in amongst the tall grass separating the woods from the dirt road.

"Grab the minnows will ya?" Al said as he carefully pulled his fishing rod from the back seat of his car. Bob did the same, while also removing the minnow bucket from the floorboards of the backseat. He placed it inside a bucket to avoid splashing around in the car. Also in the bucket was a lantern and small tackle box.

"I got a feeling we're gonna nail 'em tonight," Bob said as he followed his fishing partner off the road into the woods along a trail.

The river could be seen through the woods, only 20 yards or so to their right. They would now walk parallel to the east channel a couple hundred yards before moving over to the river's edge at the base of the wing dam.

"Yeah, with this hot, dry weather, the river should be down and clear," Al said without looking back, picking his way around trees on the sparsely worn trail. "Bet we pick up some northerns too, before the sun sets."

The trail soon came to the bank of the river. The low August water levels had left a 10 foot wide sand bar separating the woods from the water. The stretch of sandy beach was interrupted at their feet by one pile of rocks starting at the woodline and stretching into the water, the wing dam that they hoped held the structure in which they would find bass and northern pike.

"Grab me a minnow, will ya?" Al asked as he unhooked his three-eighth ounce jighead hook from the lowest eye of his fishing pole.

Bob reached into the minnow bucket and pulled out two fathead minnows, often called pike minnows by the fisherman using them for bait.

"I'll grab our chair," Bob said and stepped into the woods long enough to drag out a log, used in previous fishing trips such as this evenings.

Bob pulled the log into its spot on the downstream side of the row of rocks. Both men slid the hook from the jighead through the bottom, then top lip of the pike minnows. Then, with a flip of the wrist, each young man took turns casting upstream of the swirling water, agitated as it flowed over the line of rocks underwater. The power of the river current, even during low water levels, carried their bait downstream faster than the weighted jighead could sink. Experience had taught the 16 year olds that they should feel their leaded hooks bounce over the top of the wing dam before settling down over the top, where hungry predator fish were waiting, ready to ambush minnows coming over the top of the rocks.

Right away, Al, set the hook into a fish. His line shot downstream briefly, but Al stopped the fish's progress in no time, reeling in a largemouth bass, about a foot long.

"Not bad," Al said with a shrug, as he grasped the fish by its lower jaw and jerked the hook free.

"I've seen smaller," Bob said with a laugh, and watched his friend release the fish.

At that moment, Bob reared back, setting the hook on a fish of his own. This one jumped out of the water upon the hook set.

"Smallie!" Bob said enthusiastically, recognizing the smallmouth bass's characteristic above water acrobatics.

An hour later the young men had caught nearly two dozen fish; a mixed bag of largemouth and smallmouth bass as well as two northern pike, each around 25 inches long. The pike they kept in their bucket. The bass had been thrown back. The northern pike would make a good meal, baked by their mothers in the oven. Darkness was coming on and they now were hoping the walleye bite would come on. Walleyes were the eating fish they were looking for, and the best bite occurred just before dark and for about a half hour or so afterwards.

They weren't disappointed. Just as the sun began to go behind the trees downstream of their little sandy beach at the base of their favorite wing dam, Al set the hook into a fish, and saw the golden tint of the fish, along with the white tail of a walleye pike, fighting his line in current- a nice 15 inch walleye.

"Nice!" Bob said with a grin. "Now that's what we're looking for!"

A half hour later, the friends began their walk out of the woods in the dark, lantern in hand and a bucket of walleyes and a couple northern pike for their effort.

CHAPTER 6

***

Bob and Al swatted mosquitos as they walked through the woods to Al's car, their glowing lantern lighting their path. Soon laughing and loud voices could be heard ahead of them. As they drew closer to the open area around the chimney, they were able to make out through the darkness and trees, a fire, with the silhouettes of party goers in the firelight.

When the young men cleared the woods in the opening, a familiar shout came through the darkness from near the big fire roaring inside the old chimney.

As Bob and Al emerged from the woods,

someone yelled, "Hey you river rats!"

Al and Bob immediately knew their teammate Jim Scheel, was the loud voice coming from the fire ring. They dropped their fishing rods and gear and walked over to the group; six young men, all a little older than the young fishermen, and all out having a good time on a warm August night.

"Bob! Hey, can you believe it?! This here guy thinks Cleveland is going to win the World Series this year! Can you believe it?" yelled Cliff, pointing at Jim when Bob and Al joined the group around the fire.

"Yeah! Feller can carry that team," yelled Jim with as much enthusiasm, "And...and Lou Boudreau and Hal Trosky will provide the offense. Nobody will touch Cleveland this year!"

"You're drunk," Countered Cliff with a wave. "Now the Detroit Tigers, that's the team to beat. With Greenburg and McCosky's hitting and Newsome's pitching, the Tigers will win it all."

"You're the one who's talkin' drunk!" Yelled Jim. "Bob, Cleveland right?!"

"Boy, you guys must have been here since noon. Everybody knows the Yankees will make it five straight," Bob said with a laugh.

"I hate the Yankees!" Cliff shouted again.

"No kiddin,'" Jim added and shook his head.

The chimney was a common gathering spot for people Bob's age for several reasons. It was a secluded place, away from adults. If they were lucky, some girls may join them. And, it was on the Wisconsin side of the river. The drinking age in Minnesota was 21. In Wisconsin, you had to be 21 to drink hard alcohol....but, you could drink beer at age 18. So, Bob's friends knew that if a police officer bothered to venture down the old dirt road leading to the chimney, he would find a group of 18 year olds minding their own business, drinking beer in Wisconsin legally.

The debates and storytelling, along with the ribbing was always done in fun. The guys from McGuires were strong friends and loyal teammates. Bob and Al were the young guys on the team. They weren't joining the older guys in their weekend activities, but they never felt excluded. Their teammates were like older brothers, looking out for the younger men.

"Guys, we gotta get going," Bob interrupted the laughing and joking banter of his teammates. "We have a bucket full of walleyes and a couple northerns to fillet up."

"Bring them over here, I want to take a look!" exclaimed Tom Baab.

Al went over and grabbed the bucket, and made his way back over to the firelight. Setting the bucket down, he reached in and pulled a plump walleye out of the bucket half filled with water and fish. The walleye, still alive, flexed his golden brown body, searching for freedom from Al's grasp.

"Not too shabby," Tom said with a nod of his head.

"Where'd you get those guys from?" Jim asked.

"Off the wing dam, couple hundred yards down river," Bob said, pulling out a northern, grasping the long fish behind the head, its slime dripping off its wet sides as he lifted him free from the bucket.

"Wow! The kid can pitch AND catch fish!" Tom exclaimed.

"Well, gotta go guys, practice on Tuesday night, right?" Al said.

"Yeah, I really want to beat those guys from Wojeskis!" Bob said with conviction.

"You mean you want to beat Wojeski....the team, don't you?" a voice came from behind Bob.

Everyone stopped talking and looked beyond the firelight. Four people stepped out of the darkness and approached the group from

McGuires baseball team. It was Ed and Marie, along with Ed's catcher and friend Doug, and his girlfriend Sherry.

"You mean you want to beat the Wojeski team, don't you Bob?" Ed asked again, coming closer, standing almost on top of Bob now, a full head taller, glaring down at Bob.

Bob stared up at Ed while his friends came closer.

"I think you're taking this game a little personal, don't you?" Ed said, still addressing Bob at close range.

"That's not what I meant. I mean…we all want to win the game," Bob said in defense, his voice trying unsuccessfully to hide both fear and anger.

"I think I know why you want this game so badly," Ed continued.

"Ed, the kid didn't mean anything by it," Jim said, coming alongside Bob and trying to relieve the tension.

"I think he did!" Ed said, beginning to anger. "He said he wanted to beat the GUYS from Wojeskis!"

Now it was Al's turn to come to the defense of his pitcher. "Look, Ed, it's not wrong for Bob to want to win is it?"

"He's our best pitcher…the guy just wants to win!" Tom said sharply. "He sat in your shadow on our high school team. Now he just wants to prove himself!"

"That has nothing to do with it!" Ed shouted, turning to point his finger at Tom. "I know why he wants to win so badly, I've seen him in the bleachers at the games!" Turning back to Bob, staring menacingly, he addressed the whole group, "The grease monkey has eyes for my girl!"

Without even thinking, Bob threw a punch. Ed had been standing too close, and the only shot Bob had managed was a punch to the side of Ed's head. Then Ed had him, grabbing him by the collar of his t-shirt, pushing him backwards in the dark, holding him up, but keeping the younger man off balance. Bob's teammates were trying to grab hold of the larger, 18 year old, but Doug had joined the fray, pulling guys off Ed.

Ed stopped his charge, pulled Bob in closer, then cocked his right arm back, still holding Bob's shirt with his left hand, and threw his whole upper body into the punch.

A deep daze hit Bob, and he barely felt his body hitting the ground. His whole head hurt instantly. Looking up in the confusion of darkness, firelight, and smoke, bodies bounced around in his line of vision.

Bob was unsure how long he lay there. His head was not yet clear when he began to recognize shouts, threats, and then people were helping him up. His feet were under him, but the world kept feeling like it was trying to tip him over. His friends were saying 'hang onto him' and 'let's get him to the car'.

He was halfway across the Winona High Bridge in Al's car, when he was finally able to understand Al's questions.

"You okay Bob?" Al asked, his hand on Bob's shoulder, trying to snap him out of the fog he was in.

"Ohhh, my head hurts," Bob finally said.

"Wow! You have to get a hand up or something. He really clobbered you a good one!" Al said with a chuckle.

"Yeah, I couldn't block his punch, he had me off balance," Bob said with his head in his hands, slumping some in the passenger seat, now beginning to feel embarrassed by his rapid defeat. "Well, your teammates ran him and Doug off," Al said confidently, laughing. "You sure better pitch good next weekend, is all I can say."

CHAPTER 7

***

Bob wasn't sure which bruise hurt the most, the one encompassing his left eye, or the one on his ego. He had a glimpse of victory in his fight with Ed, only to see it extinguished with one punch. He was glad he wasn't too coherent when Al helped him to his car. He wouldn't have wanted to see everyone looking at him. He was also glad Ed had left before his friends helped him to his feet. He was especially relieved Marie wasn't there to see his friends practically carry him to Al's car.

As he lay in bed Sunday morning, his

thoughts, usually focused on which fishing spot to try that day, now swirled with anxiety about next week's game. There was a lot at stake. Team pride was a big factor. Being the pitcher on his town baseball team, his performance could make or break the game. He had off games before, and his team had lost. All season he had been solid, consistent, in control of his pitches and his emotions. If he lost focus, walked a batter or two, he had always been able to get back on track, remain calm, and get out of a tough inning. This game was different. The last time his team had lost in league play was against Wojeskis. That was last year in the championship game, before he joined the team.

As he lay in bed petting his lab Duke, who had hopped into bed with him, he began to think about that game and see the connection with how he felt just before the fight the previous night.

What was it about Ed Wojeski that turned him into a wreck? Ed was a strong, successful, competitive guy, but that shouldn't have messed Bob up so much. He's played ball against guys like Ed before-good ball players with good jobs who wanted to win. Bob knew what it was. He had known it for some time. He just hadn't come to grips with it until it got punched into him. It was Marie. Ed knew it too. He made that clear last night, just before punching his lights out.

Ed was right. Bob was jealous of Ed's success, of his ability on the ball field, and of his girlfriend.

CHAPTER 8

***

"Nice shiner," Buzz said flatly when Bob rolled into the garage on Monday morning. Nic looked up from his work bench inquisitively, and then went back to his papers, getting ready to start the day.

"Bob, you can get on that Ford there," Nic said without looking up.

Following his drive to be as efficient as possible, Nic was always the first to arrive at the garage. His first task was always to tape a work order to each vehicle in the garage. He always taped it to the top part of the vehicle's cab, where the top of the automobile met the windshield. When Bob and Buzz arrived, they didn't have to waste time checking with their father, they just had to walk over to the vehicle and look at the work order. The Ford was a 1932 Model 18, and like other Model 18's from that year, it needed a new starter switch. Bob had done this replacement over a dozen times, and dove into his work.

The whole week consisted of working at the garage, going home, and working out. Bob stayed as long as he could at the garage each day finding extra things to do, clean, and organize. If he stayed busy with work, he knew he'd have an excuse when Al or Cliff would stop by and want to go out with some of the other guys. He also knew if he did go with the guys, he would run the risk of running into Ed somewhere. He wasn't afraid of a physical confrontation, but he couldn't help but feeling embarrassed by his loss in his brief battle with Ed on Saturday night.

When he went home each night no earlier than 7:00 P.M., he would have a quick dinner and lift some weights in the basement. Then, under the cover of darkness, he'd go for a five mile run with Duke, anxious to get out and move. Bob headed for the river. From their house, he only needed to run six blocks until he hit the levee, the concrete road and embankment where riverboats and other water craft could tie up. From there he turned and headed up river until the road turned toward the industrial park along the river, where barges were loaded and unloaded. He could now stop momentarily to let Duke off his leash. The minimal traffic on the road allowed the opportunity for the black lab to run alongside Bob, darting down the embankment to the river occasionally when he got a whiff of something worth investigating.

The run was great exercise. But, it also gave him a chance to think. His desire to win Friday night's game was nearly overwhelming. He knew he'd have to face Ed at least a couple times during the game. He visualized the encounter. What pitches he would throw, whether Ed would chase his curveball, whether he dared try to sneak a fastball past him. What would everyone's reaction be if his team won....or if they lost? Would Marie be there? Of course she would.

All the scenarios swirled in his head as he ran.

A little bit of razzing from the guys on the team on Tuesday and Thursday night about his black eye was okay, but he was trying his best to concentrate on Friday night's game against Wojeskis.

CHAPTER 9

***

All week long, the sports section of the Winona Republican-Herald had articles discussing Friday's championship game. One headline referred to the matchup between Graham and McGuires and Wojeskis as the 'Kingpins of area baseball'. The article went on to say that 'The hustling Graham and McGuires-the boys with winged feet, were going against the hard hitting boys from Wojeskis Stone'.

The hype continued all week in the paper, often referring to the high school baseball team where Ed recently graduated, and how he was the mentor for the young pitcher, Bob. Bob laughed a bit about that one. They were high school teammates, but not exactly on good terms, and he certainly didn't look at Ed as his mentor. Their relationship was probably more competitive than it should have been.

Nic was noticeably agitated as people kept popping into the garage at random times to ask Bob if he was nervous, how his arm felt, or if he was going to avenge last year's loss. Bob didn't mind taking a moment or two away from the car he was working on to talk with people, especially if they were customers, but Nic wasn't always too easy going about people interfering with the work that had to be done.

"Just make sure you get your work done," Nic told his son during a lunch break on Wednesday.

The game was Friday night at 7:00 P.M. Bob's team met at 5:00 to take some batting practice. Wojeskis could be seen on another field nearby on the string of ballfields bordering Lake Winona.

Bob took his time warming up his arm, throwing with Al. His teammates were quieter than usual, not laughing and joking around like they usually do during practice. This game was for the league title and everyone was trying to stay focused.

However, Bob was struggling to stay focused. While he and his teammates took their cuts in batting practice, he couldn't help looking to the other field and seeing the Wojeski players hit long fly balls, some clearing the fence. His Graham and McGuires team was put together differently than Wojeskis. His team was built for speed. They were a line drive hitting bunch, trying to hit shots in the gap and taking extra bases when they could. They used good base running and hustle to manufacture runs, instead of relying on the long ball.

It took forever for the game to finally start. The bleachers were full of fans from Winona and neighboring Minnesota City. The guys began to fire up and talk more, feeling the excitement of the big game and a crowd of over 500, watching. Bob tried to concentrate on being fired up with his teammates, avoiding looking over at the Wojeski team, not wanting to make eye contact with Ed.

Bob's team took the field first. He was sharp right away, getting the first three batters out on two fly ball outs and a weak ground ball back to Bob and an easy throw to first. A sense of relief hit him as he jogged back to the dugout, the butterflies starting to leave him.

It was Ed who struggled to start the game. He

struggled to find the plate, and the McGuires guys were patient, getting ahead of Ed on the pitch count, waiting for a good pitch.

For McGuires in the bottom of the first, Wilbur Winblad started the game by dropping a bloop single back of second base. He went to second on one of Ed's wild pitches, and took third on a passed ball to the backstop. Bill Corcoran was safe on an error and Winblad dashed home with the first run. Ed struck out Jim, but Tom drove a double to the fence that put Bob's teammates on second and third. Ed finally settled down and struck out the next two guys to retire the side.

In the top of the second inning, the butterflies came back. Ed was going to lead off the inning. Bob could feel the big man's eyes on him as he took his practice swings and Bob took his warm up pitches. Cheers erupted as Ed stepped to the plate and dug in. Bob then watched as his first pitch was lined into left center field for a base hit. A glance over to first base to keep Ed close was met by no emotion from Ed, hands on his knees leading off, all business. His presence on the base paths was short lived as a couple pitches later, his buddy Doug hit a ground ball in the hole to short, and Ed was forced at second base. Bob retrieved the ball and smoothed the dirt on the mound, head down, as Ed jogged past him and back into his dugout. A strikeout and a ground ball out and McGuires was out of the inning.

In the bottom of the second inning, the McGuires team turned a walk, a stolen base, and a base hit into another run. The third inning was also quick, with Bob giving up a base hit in the top and McGuires manufacturing another run to make it 3-0 going into the fourth inning.

Bunts were dropping all over the infield for McGuires in the bottom of the fourth. Bob came to bat to lead off the inning, now well into the rhythm of the game, ignoring the fact he was facing his nemesis and dropped a bunt down, digging hard to beat the throw to first. Ed kept close tabs on him at first, looking over as Bob took a healthy lead. By now, Bob's focus was on the game, concentrating on Ed's movements, trying to read his delivery to home, careful not to get picked off first base. Winblad followed suit, laying down another bunt. Bob knew the bunt was coming and was stealing on the pitch, giving him the chance to round second hard and slide into third, with Winblad safe at first on the throw. Both runners scored on a deep single by Stan Smith. Two more McGuires singles and another costly error by Wojeskis and the score was now 7-0.

The next two innings flew by with both teams threatening to score but coming up empty. The top of seventh came and both pitchers were showing signs of fatigue. The August air was heavy and the temperature was high. Things began to fall apart for Bob in the seventh.

Ned Turner led off with a single. Bob's velocity had begun to fall off, which in turn made his changeup less effective. A costly error at second ruined an easy double play, and now runners stood on first and third with no outs.

Ed now came to the plate, already two for two for the game. Bob dug around the pitcher's mound trying to relax, taking deep breaths when a comforting hand was placed on his shoulder. It was Cliff, his shortstop, making another one of his timely visits to the mound, trying to calm down his young pitcher.

"Just relax, Buddy," Cliff said with a soft confidence. "This next guy will hit another ground ball, we won't mess it up this time. We'll turn the double play and not worry about the run. Just do your thing…we're behind you."

"Thanks," Bob said and turned his attention back to the batter.

Ed quickly stepped back into the box and readied himself for the pitch. The next two pitches were balls, curve balls starting out in the strike zone, but curving out at the last moment. Ed didn't bite. Ed connected on the third pitch, a grounder up the middle that Bob lunged at. Missing, the ball continued bounding up the middle, but Stan made a diving stop, and from his back flipped the ball to second for an out. Ed, running hard, beat the relay to first and was safe. The runner scored and the score was 7 to 1.

Bob felt a bit of relief, but that was short lived. Two batters later, a walk and a single, and Bob was facing bases loaded with only one out.

The young pitcher took a moment and walked around the mound, wiping the sweat from his brow and rubbing on the baseball.

Shouts from the crowd and from his teammates rose in volume, "Come on Bob!"..."Let's go Bobby!"..."You got this guy!"

The next pitch was to Clay Garvin, Wojeski's first baseman. The big man swung hard and deposited the ball over the center field fence for a grand slam homerun. Just like that the score was now 7 to 5.

Bob dropped his head in disgust, slamming his fist into his glove. He watched the guys from

Wojeskis circle the bases and the ensuing celebration at home as McGuires infielders and Al, from behind the plate, jogged to the mound. For the first time during the game, Bob searched the crowd. Marie immediately came to his mind. He had a chance to impress….was it her he wanted to impress, his father, who he just spotted sitting with his mother, Buzz, and sister Esther. Maybe it was his father he wanted to impress.

Almost as if he were reading his mind, Al pulled him close with his muscular arm and spoke to the young pitcher just loud enough for him to hear, "You can get us out of this Bob. You can take us the rest of the way. Don't worry about what others think. You're not here to gain their respect. We have plenty of that for you. Win for you and your teammates."

His team gathered around him now as well, arms went around his shoulder as his older teammates encouraged him…reassured him that he could get through the inning.

"Okay, okay," Bob said as his teammates smacked him on the back and hustled back to their positions, shouting, "Let's go!" and smacking their mitts.

Bob pitched a bit more cautiously to the next batter, knowing that his fastball had waned. A fly ball out and a ground out to third got McGuires off the field and into the dugout, relieved that they still clung to a two run lead.

The Graham and McGuires team did what they do the best in the bottom of the seventh inning. They turned a single into a run with a stolen base, advancing a runner on a ground out, and a sacrifice fly. On the mound, Bob continued to tire and his control had begun to falter, walking one batter and throwing a lot of pitches in the inning, throwing a lot of curveballs and allowing the batters to go deep into the count. Wojeskis managed to get one run back to make it 8 to 6 going into the bottom of the 8th.

Bob was hoping for some insurance runs in the bottom of the 8th.

"How ya doing?" Jim asked, when they were back in the dugout.

"I'm alright," Bob said, trying to sound convincing. He was tired, but he was almost to the end. There was no way he was going to exit the game now.

"It's your game Buddy!" Jim said and slapped him on the back.

"Hopefully we can get us a cushion," Tom said, and grabbed a bat, heading to the on deck circle.

The young men from McGuires wanted to win just as much as Bob, but no more runs came from them in the bottom of the eighth, and Bob and his teammates jogged out for the 9th.

With a two run lead, Bob tried to be careful, but his extra caution led to a leadoff walk. McGuires outfielders then chased down two fly balls for outs, both nearly dropping in the gap in left center field. With two outs, sweat rolled off Bob as he worked to control his anxiety, taking deep breaths as the next batter stepped to the plate. A soft line drive on the next pitch dropped in for a single, moving the runner to third.

With runners at the corners and two outs, the next Wojeski batter dug in with Ed standing on deck. The crowd cheered, knowing the game was coming down to the wire.

Al pumped his fist from behind the plate, "Come on Bob! This is your guy, right here!"

Bob's first pitch was a changeup, hoping to get the anxious batter to reach for a low pitch, out of the strike zone. Ball one. His next pitch was his curve that started over the plate, but dove outside. This time the batter was fooled and swung and missed. Bob glanced into the on deck circle to see big Ed, rubbing the barrel of his bat, watching Bob intently. With a one and one count, Bob came in high and tight with a fastball. The batter tried to stop his swing, but it was too late, his check swing popped straight up. Al threw off his catcher's mask, looked up, found the ball, and squeezed it for the final out.

The Graham and McGuire baseball team had won. Ed would not get his chance to win the game. Bob and his teammates celebrated around Al at home plate.

November 11th, 1940
Armistice Day

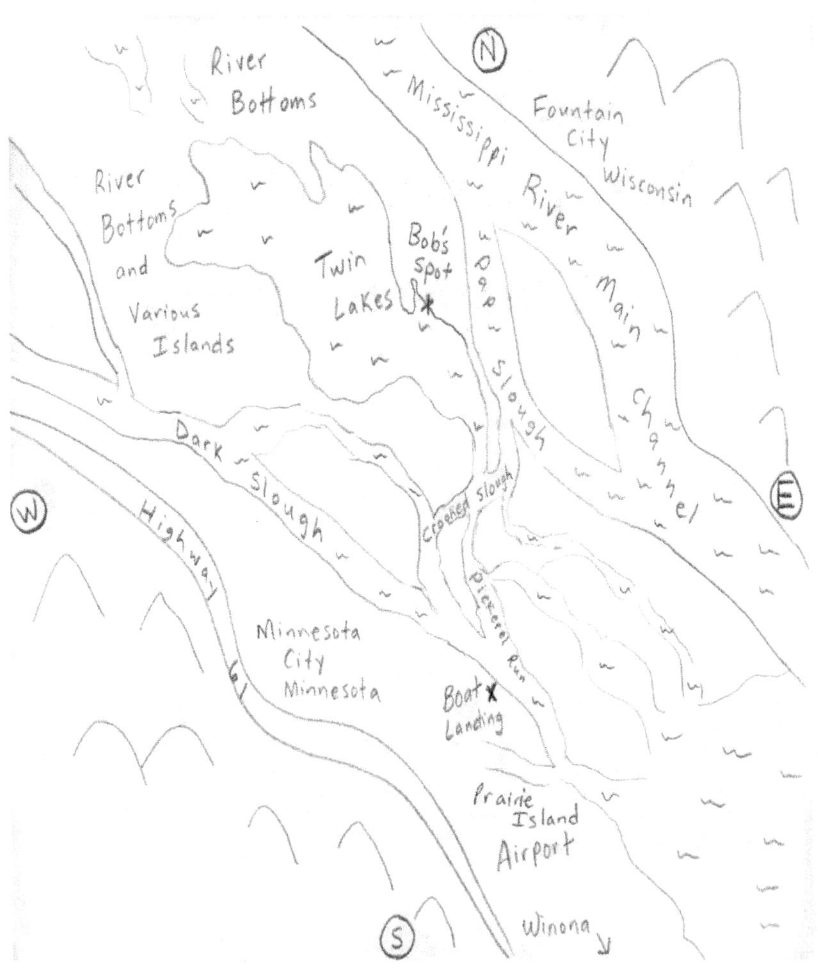
River
Bottoms
N
Mississippi
River
Main
Channel
Fountain
City
Wisconsin
River
Bottoms
and
Various
Islands
Twin
Lakes
Bob's
Spot
Slough
Dark
Slough
Crooked Slough
E
W
Highway
61
Pickerel Run
Minnesota
City
Minnesota
Boat
Landing
Prairie
Island
Airport
S
Winona

CHAPTER 11

***

The alarm went off at 4:00 A.M. and Bob was quick to climb out of bed. It was a Monday, November 11th, Armistice Day, the day celebrating the end of World War I. Schools were closed in recognition of the holiday, but Nic knew people may take advantage of having a day off of work and bring their car in. Nic hoped his shrewd thinking would make him some money today. Work had piled up at the garage, and his father and Buzz were planning to get caught up. His father had told him that if he helped out, they would go after ducks later. Their goal was to get an early start, wrap up the work by late morning, noon at the latest, then head to Twin Lakes for the afternoon and evening hunt.

"This is a reward for a good first quarter report card," his father told him as they drove to the garage in the early morning darkness.

"I understand," Bob replied with a grin.

He knew the report card was just his father's way of justifying taking a day, or at least a part of the day to go hunting when there was work that could be done.

It probably wouldn't be a perfect day to hunt anyway. Not much wind and the temperatures could get into the 50's, maybe even flirt with 60. Not a great day for duck hunting, but any day hunting was a good day.

The hunters in the area had been waiting for a cold front to push the ducks down from the Dakotas and Canada, to get the northern birds moving south. The hunting season had consisted of too many blue bird days so far, mostly clear skies and warm temperatures. The majority of the migration was still up north.

Buzz joined Bob and their father around 6:00 A.M.

"I can't believe you actually beat me to work," Buzz said with a smirk and shake of his head.

"I'm just trying to help you guys get caught

up," Bob told his brother, who had taken to ignoring his younger brother, popping the hood on a Plymouth.

The morning dragged on while the men tried to get through the cars waiting for repair. For November, the weather was so balmy that both garage bay doors were opened early on in the morning.

"Too warm for duck hunting anyway," Buzz said as he stepped outside to pull another car in for a new muffler.

"Beats sittin' at school!" Bob fired back.

About 9:30, Bob scooted out from under a car to find his father standing over him with his arms folded.

"Son," Nic said with a frown and shake of his head, "I'm not sure I'm going to make it hunting. I got more cars coming in than going out. I can't turn anybody away and hate to leave it all for Buzz. I promised you duck hunting today, so if you want to head out when you're done with this one, go ahead.

"If it's okay, I guess I could," Bob said trying to sound disappointed, masking his excitement while inserting a slightly guilty tone. "What will Mom say?"

"She'll be fine with it," his father said.

A half hour later, Bob was taking his father's truck back home to pick up the boat and Duke. He knew his father felt bad. Nic tried hard to please everyone. Yet sometimes pleasing his sons by spending time with them took a backseat to his garage and his customers. It was just his way.

Bob figured, he'd try to help out every evening the rest of the week as late as he could, to help his father and Buzz catch up.

"Get in boy," Bob said to his dog, while loading his gear into the truck, and turned to load his dog, growing more excited by the moment.

Duke knew where he was going and no matter how often he hunted, once the gun and hunting clothes came out, he was wired, bouncing around excitedly. Bob could scarcely clean his gun during the off season without Duke working himself into a frenzy.

Bob began pulling out of the driveway, looking back instinctively to see that his trailered boat was clearing the tree next to the driveway.

Bob stopped his truck, scrunched up his mouth thinking, "Better grab my dry bag just in case," he said to himself as much as to Duke, sitting next to him in the truck.

Quickly Bob ducked back into the garage and grabbed his two foot long durable plastic bag, sealed tight with a bungee cord in which he kept an extra sweatshirt, sweatpants, gloves, and a stocking cap. He figured he wouldn't need it, but it never hurt to have some extra clothes along.

"Hey! Shouldn't you be doing some homework?" yelled his neighbor Sonny Ehlers coming out his back door.

"Yeah," Bob said with a laugh, "but, first I figured I'd go scare some birds."

"I've seen you shoot, scarin' them is about all you do!" Sonny laughed.

"Well, I don't have school today, and Dad said if I helped him at the garage this morning, he's take me out, but he's still too busy, so he said to go without him," Bob said feeling guilty. "Besides, looks like you have the same plan," Bob said pointing to the cased gun in Sonny's hand.

"Also guilty!" Sonny said with a laugh. "Norman Roloff and I are headed up to Read's Landing to give it a shot. Ducks gotta fly sometime. Jeez, it's 50 degrees in mid-November. Ducks can't stay up north forever."

"Well, good luck!" Bob said to his neighbor, and tossed the dry bag into the floor of his truck in front of Duke, sitting calmly now that he knew he wasn't going to be missing out on the action.

Bob pulled the rest of the way out of his

driveway and headed down the street, boat in tow toward Broadway, then west through town, and out onto Prairie Island.

"Hopefully we'll have some birds moving today," Bob said to his dog, reaching out to rustle the dark fur on the back of Duke's neck.

The route Bob drove was the same as his running course, along a short stretch of river, then out onto Prairie Island. Prairie Island was not really an island, but rather a strip of dry ground wedged between the Mississippi backwater and a series of marshes, replenished with water each year from the spring floods. Other hunters pulling boats could be seen ahead and behind Bob as he drove.

Some would drop their small boats or canoes into the marsh, hunting the shorelines of the several mile long series of shallow strips of marsh. The majority of the hunters would put in just north of Winona at a couple different landings and hunt the backwater sloughs of the main channel of the Mississippi.

At Vercoda Landing only two vehicles were ahead of him, sliding their 12 or 14 foot aluminum boats off their trailers into the water. Bob sat in his truck and waited his turn. Two boats could be put in at once at Vercoda Landing. Two gravel runways angled into the water providing the ramp for vehicle and trailer, with a dock stretching out into the water between.

While waiting, Bob watched a pair of older hunters trailering their boat, done hunting for the day. Their dog, a golden retriever, ran over to Bob's truck, placing his paws on the passenger side to greet Duke. Duke's whole body wagged in greeting. The men, probably in their mid-60's, worked to load their boat, one winching the boat on the trailer, while the other sat in the truck, ready to pull forward.

As the older hunter pulled the trailer and boat free of the water, he briefly stopped alongside Bob's truck and rolled his window down.

"Could be crowded out there today," the man, gray whiskers tainted with tobacco juice, said with a grin, nodding toward the line of vehicles pulling boats now beginning to line up behind Bob, waiting for their turn to launch their craft.

"Yeah, looks like you guys called it quits for the day!" Bob replied politely.

"Nothing flying," the man said with a disappointed wave. "Good luck!" he then said and continued on up the boat ramp.

As the man pulled his trailer past him, Bob quickly swung his truck ahead and positioned the trailer at the foot of the ramp. Since he was alone, he had to work fast. The hunters waiting in line would often grow impatient with a slow moving hunter at the ramp, taking too long to launch his boat. Bob unstrapped his boat from the trailer quickly, throwing his dry bag into the boat as well. Duke vacated the truck and ran onto the dock to visit with another hunter's dog, who had now jumped into the water alongside the dock.

Bob quickly tied a long rope onto the bumper of his truck, and backed it into the water. The boat slid off clean, stopping as it cleared the back of the trailer. The rope on the truck, the other end on the eye hook on the front of the boat, halted the boat as it entered the water free of the trailer. As quickly as possible, Bob jumped back out of his truck and used the rope to pull the boat to the sandy edge of the landing, out of the way of the next boat preparing to be launched. Bob untied the rope from his truck, tossed it in a heap in front of the boat and drove his truck to the little parking lot. His launch had been so quick, he caught up with the older gentlemen, who had stopped up the ramp to apply tie down straps to their boat and trailer, as he jogged back down the slope of the boat launch.

"Might rain later," another hunter said,

scrambling into his boat, "Hopefully we'll see more birds. Good luck to you!"

"You too!" Bob replied as he coiled his rope quickly and whistled for Duke, who quickly leaped in the boat just as Bob shoved the boat free from shore.

Climbing to the back of his boat, he choked the motor, gave the cord a pull, and was rewarded with the smoky roar as his Evinrude came to life.

Hunters were always social. Small talk at the boat landing wasn't uncommon. Most guys were tolerant and patient of one another while loading and unloading their boats. Many of the hunters were regulars, especially the older guys. Bob would often see the same guys and dogs every time he went.

Within a minute he was cruising along Pickerel Run. Usually when he went out, he would be a bit more cautious, since he would have to use his flashlight in the predawn darkness to spot the white channel markers, alerting hunters of stumps or submerged rock piles, waiting to rip the lower units out of boat motors. But going out in the middle of the day, he could run his little boat at a steady clip, and not worry about picking his way through the narrow channel and its obstacles.

Turning into Twin Lakes, Bob took a quick look at his watch. 11:50 A.M. He would have a good six hours to hunt. The skies were blue and a light breeze felt almost damp, giving the November day somewhat of a balmy feel.

Duke, perched up front, took a face full of water as the boat bounced into the larger waves on the bigger piece of water, and retreated to the middle of the boat, seeking shelter at Bob's feet and behind the decoy bag. Other hunters began to appear, standing up in their boats, rising above the cattails and marsh grass, so Bob would see them and not pull into their spots.

Hunters were territorial. The rule was 'keep your distance, 100 yards if possible', to give everybody clear shooting and room for the ducks to swing into the decoys. Hunters who pulled ashore too close to another hunter better be ready for an argument, or sometimes even a physical confrontation. Fights out on the marsh were not unheard of. If a flock of ducks were responding to a hunter's hail call, or a spread of decoys, banking in their flight to land into the wind, another hunter better not take shots.

Bob idled his boat, 30 yards from the little point of his bay. Standing in his boat, he began placing a decoy spread, an arc of a dozen or so mallards, each anchored by a chord and weight. Starting in the bay a bit, Bob unwound each decoy and tossed it in the water. Duke leaned over the edge of the boat, his feet on the rail, resisting his urge to jump in after each bobbing decoy, as Bob continued his semi-circle to the point of the little strip of island separating his bay from the rougher waters of Twin Lakes.

Satisfied with his decoy spread, Bob began driving his boat toward the shore. As he neared the cattails and marsh grass coming from the water, he gunned the motor a little to push his way throw the vegetation, somewhat anchoring the boat, still in the water a yard or so from shore. The dense water plants would stabilize his boat for the shooting to come.

Bob cut his motor and Duke jumped into the water and leapt ashore, disappearing into the narrow strip of woods.

"Not here buddy," Bob said to himself upon hearing another boat approach. Like the other hunters he saw earlier, Bob stood high on his seat and waved his arm at the passing boat. The other boat continued past the bay as Bob sat down and traded his knee high rubber boots for his chest waders, which had been under his decoy bag.

Bob was busy bending some marsh grass over

the gunwhale of his boat, and about to load his Winchester Model 12, when Duke bounded back into the boat, done exploring the woods and was ready to hunt.

"Welcome back," Bob said to his dog, defending himself from the spraying water as Duke shook the water off him, "Did you make sure we have the place to ourselves this morning?"

Waders on, Bob scanned the decoy spread one last time, making sure all were upright and no lines crossed the back of a decoy, a mistake that could cause weary late season mallards, used to being shot at, to flair.

Bob was hoping the older gentleman at the boat landing was right about rain moving in later. He hoped the wind would pick up a bit more as well. A little wind and rain would push the ducks into the calmer bays, giving him some good shooting. The rain would keep their flight low. Right now, the skies were blue and the wind was light at the most. He settled in for what looked to be a long boring day, kicking his feet up on the side of his boat, gun in his lap, Duke sitting at the back of the boat, scanning the blue skies for ducks that weren't there.

CHAPTER 12

***

By 2:00, the rain that the old hunter had predicted had begun to fall, and with it came some wind, gusty at first, but becoming steady as the rain came down a little harder. Bob had put his rain coat on a little while earlier, but now the wind had a hint of cooler air with it, and Bob zipped it up tight.

Two hours of sitting in his boat without seeing anything more than a couple high flying flocks, had just changed. A flock of a dozen mallards flying low across Twin Lakes, responded to his hail call, and banked toward the mouth of the bay.

Bob switched to a feeding call, and the birds locked their wings into the wind and began to settle into the pocket created by the arcing string of decoys. Even in the growing wind and rain, Bob picked out a drake and squeezed off three shots just as they were about to touchdown in the water, dropping two birds. Duke sprang into the water. Within a minute, Duke had retrieved one bird and was headed back for the second. Bob had just enough time to admire the drake mallard and Duke was back, huffing as he swam with a hen clenched in his mouth. Bob grabbed the duck, then shedding a glove, reached overboard and hoisted Duke back into the boat.

"Nice job boy!" Bob praised his roommate and tossed him a cookie.

Bob was amazed at how quickly the weather could change in October and November in Minnesota. It was now 3:15 P.M., and the weather had rapidly turned colder. The ducks had been pretty scarce until about the last 20 minutes. It seemed almost too sudden to believe. The duck hunting went from nearly boring to fast and furious action as quickly as the weather changed. Large flocks could be seen heading from upriver, flying low and fast in the wind, as if pushed by the frigid north wind.

Bob had just dropped another drake mallard, and as Duke was jumping in for his retrieve, Bob swung quickly on another flock of over two dozen mallards and dropped another. Duke was trying to make head way against the wind and waves, but was having trouble making any progress. The waves were breaking at their peak, the white foam crashing onto Duke's head every time he crested a wave. His reaction was to shake his head each time, which slowed any momentum he had. And, to compound matters, the rain, merely a soft rain on a balmy day only hours earlier, had turned to snow, blowing in sideways and hindering Bob's view of his dog.

Bob struggled to see the ducks as they were out of sight more than visible. He figured Duke was heading toward where they splashed down, rather than having any visual on them.

"Tweet!" Bob blasted into his whistle, trying to turn Duke to the right and get him back on track for the retrieve.

Duke was getting nowhere now, the crest of each wave nearly pushing the young dog upright in the water, unable to gain any ground.

The young lab had been out in the water now for several minutes, not that long for Duke on a normal day. Many a day, Bob had thrown a retrieving dummy for Duke as far as he could out into the main channel and watched Duke swim out, make his retrieve, and turn around to swim back to shore. The main channel of the Mississippi River was powerful, millions of gallons a second pushing toward the gulf. By the time Duke made it to shore, he was usually 100 yards downstream. But Duke always scrambled out of the water and charged full speed, his trophy clutched in his teeth, down the sandy shoreline to drop the dummy obediently at Bob's feet.

But today was unlike any day Bob had ever seen. The weather had changed suddenly and the ducks just showed up as if someone had opened a big cage upriver. He also had never before seen such waves in the backwaters. The wind grew stronger by the minute.

Bob could not wait any longer. He hurriedly pushed his boat out of the rushes, and, trying to shelter his eyes from the now forming sleet and snow, put his knee on the bow and crawled in. Looking past the back of his boat he could now see that Duke was in real trouble. He floundered in the water, his head being submerged by each crashing wave. Scrambling over his seats to the rear of his boat, Bob raised the lever on top of his Evinrude to choke the motor. A quick pull of the cord found that he could only get a half a pull. Bob paused a moment, waiting for the cord to recoil back into the motor, but the rope stayed put. A couple short, swift yanks of the rope yielded no result.

Bob yelled into the wind, his swearing barely audible.

He had no time to remove the motor cover and feed the cord back in. Besides, he thought, it was probably caked full of ice. Looking up he realized a moment of panic when he didn't spot Duke. He stood up in the boat, a shiver running through his body. Then he saw him, being tossed across the top of a wave. Grabbing his oars, Bob quickly dropped the pins in the oar locks and jumped into the middle seat. With one big pull on the oars he crashed the rear of the boat through a wave and into the open water. Water slammed hard against the transom and lifeless motor and poured into the boat. With one arm pulling on an oar and one arm pushing he managed to spin his boat, nearly flipping it on the downward side of a wave. Bracing his legs against the seat ahead of him, he pulled on the oars with all his might and felt the empty front of the boat lurch upward on a wave. As it slid down the other side he managed to gain a bearing on Duke.

In less than a minute, a minute that seemed too long, he managed to pull alongside his dog, nearly crashing the bow into the exhausted lab. Never before had Bob seen such panic in his dog's eyes, his head still being submerged with each crashing wave. Bob released the oars and lunged over the side, managing to grab the fur on Duke's back. Clinging to fur and flesh, Bob reached farther out, nearly tossing the boat over and got an arm around the dog's neck. With one arm on Duke's collar, and leaning back with all his might, he grabbed the rim of the boat seat and pulled. Gaining a better hold, he pinned Duke's body, not struggling any more, to the side of the water filled boat. On his knees now, Bob reached both arms under Duke's belly and lifted him aboard. Duke splashed into the bottom of the boat. Bob grabbed the big dog's head and looked into his eyes, fearing the worst. The dog looked back at him with a sad, exhausted stare.

"Hang in there, Buddy," Bob said softly, hating to let go of Duke in the cold water, nearly a foot deep in the boat.

With the half submerged boat being slammed against each and every wave, Bob again scrambled to the back to try the motor again. Maybe he could get it to start with only a half pull. He grabbed the wooden end of the limp two feet of cord and bracing himself against the rocking of the boat gave it a pull. The next thing he knew he was laying in the bottom of the boat next to Duke, with the cord broken off in his hand.

Again, Bob cut loose with a volley of curses.

"We'll get you in Duke!" Bob said to his dog, the frustration and anger welling up and evident in his shouts.

He sat in the middle again, taking only a moment to slide Duke's head against the side of the boat to keep it above the water and again leaned into the oars to pull the sluggish boat with the waves, heading toward the bulrushes where they came from. With the wind at the back of the boat this time, he hoped to make better time. With the weight of all the water of the boat, and the fact that each wave was filling it more, he prayed that he would get it in before sinking. But, with some hard pulling of the oars and some angry cussing at the wind, Bob rammed the heavy boat into the rice and bulrushes.

"Come here," Bob croaked, gasping for his breath against the wind, snow, and hard work, as he picked up the dog from the bottom of the boat and stumbled to the front, closer to shore. With all the weight, the boat didn't make it all the way to shore, but struck bottom a good five feet from shore. So Bob had to jump in, with Duke still in his arms and wade the remaining distance, where he dropped to his knees, half dropping Duke onto dry land. Duke half moaned, half growled as he tried to roll onto his feet, before lying on his side, breathing hard. Bob, satisfied that his dog was still alive, at least for now, lay back in the mud and snow for a moment to catch his breath.

CHAPTER 13

***

Only a few seconds had passed, when Bob sat back up. The wind was in his face, and he thought he heard a motor. He stood up to see over the rushes and from his right, saw a boat carrying two hunters, in the lake about 75 yards from him, fighting their way through the waves. Bob knew right away that they were trying to cross Twin Lakes to get to Pickerel Run. But the wind was straight out of the east, and the two hunters had to head south to get to the entrance of the slough. They were unable to tackle the waves head on, and were forced to angle through them. Bob raised his arm to his forehead, trying to shield his eyes from the blowing snow, trying to see who they were. Like his wild ride only moments earlier, he could tell that they were taking on water, often burying the nose of their boat into the waves. Their motor was sputtering, and they weren't going very fast, fighting their way in the rough water. Then, just like that, a bad angle through the waves, maybe someone shifted their weight in the boat; the hunters' boat lurched hard and slowed, taking on water over the back.

Bob could see one man using his hands to bail, while the other worked the motor, trying to steer them into the waves now. They were going under.

Bob looked down to see that Duke was still panting, hopefully a good sign and decided he had no choice, he had to help these guys. He splashed back into the water to his boat and digging his heels in, pulled hard on the bow to bring it closer to shore. Without his weight in it, he was able to move it a little shallower. Now to get the water out. With a quick glance at the boat in the lake, a bit closer now, being pushed in with the wind, he pushed his way through the rushes to the back of his boat and pushed hard while lifting to get it as much on dry land as possible. Another glance through the blinding snow saw water pouring into the 14 foot skiff; the pair of hunters working hard to bail water with their hands, their shouts heard through the wind. Bob shuffled to the side of his own 14 footer and bending his knees and grabbing a side rail, lifted the side of the boat as high as he could. The strain was incredible at first, but as water dumped over the opposite side, the weight of the water-filled boat diminished and Bob was able to tilt the boat over sideways farther.

"Good enough," Bob gasped to himself.

As Bob took hold of the bow he looked again at the hunters. Through the waves, he saw that the men were now in the water, rising and falling in the rolling waves, clinging to the boat which had now gone upside down. Bob had to time the waves this time. Going out after Duke only minutes earlier, Bob remembered that when he pushed his boat backwards in the water, the waves were sure to fill his boat again, water pouring over the back end. As soon as a wave hit his motor....he pushed hard, trying to send his boat afloat without taking on too much water. Bob leapt in and cranked hard on one oar, spinning it around quickly to face the waves head on.

"Hang on! On my way!" Bob shouted

through the wind to the hunters.

Each cresting wave nearly launched Bob overboard as he rowed hard toward the men. The hunters looked toward Bob, seeing him now, still struggling to hang on in the wind, waves, and snow.

Bob eased his boat, now filling again from the crashing waves, alongside the men, careful not to crash into them in the rough water.

"Can you grab on?!" Bob shouted at the men.

Both men were obviously freezing. Neither man had gloves on, but both had wool caps, soaking wet, and drooping over their eyes. Bob recognized one man. It was Bruce from Wojeskis baseball team. Bruce clung to the boat, barely above water, perhaps saved by some trapped air underneath. He looked terrified. The other man, with his back to Bob clung to the near side of the boat. Bob, realizing that neither man was going to let go of their watercraft, dropped the oars again, this time lunging to grab a hunter in the same manner he only minutes earlier had grabbed Duke. A wave pushed Bob's skiff close enough to the other boat, and Bob grabbed the man's jacket.

"Let go! I have you!" Bob shouted.

The man did not respond, but after a moment let go. Bob then adjusted his grip, grabbing him under the arms, and like his efforts in rescuing Duke, braced his legs and heaved the man into the boat. Immediately Bob stepped over the man and grabbed the oars, attempting to swing his boat around to grab Bruce. His boat struck the sinking skiff as a wave slammed him sideways and Bob nearly went overboard. As he managed to come alongside Bruce, Bob was shocked at the look on his face. Bruce looked white as a ghost. He peered at Bob, expressionless now, and watched as Bob grabbed his arm and pulled him free of his grip on the sinking vessel. Bob grabbed the back of his jacket, then the back of his pants and pulled him aboard.

Like Duke, previously, both men lay in the bottom of his boat, lifeless, soaking wet, and rocking about in the half filled skiff. Bob redirected his boat and headed for shore. He looked down momentarily and saw that Bruce had closed his eyes. The other man had his face buried against the side of the boat, trying to keep his head out of the water. Neither man spoke.

As Bob neared shore he looked for an open spot in the bulrushes from which he came. He saw it and headed for the gap, pulling hard to drive his boat through and beach it. He saw Duke, still lying down, but relieved to see the dog lift his head to watch him come in. Water lurched forward in the boat as he hit shore. Bruce's head began slipping under the water in the boat, and Bob quickly grabbed him to keep his face out of the water. He jumped out of the boat, dragged Bruce out, and hauled him to shore, lying him down next to Duke. He then went back to grab the other man. He grabbed him by his coat until he could get his arms around the big man's chest and dragged him out. Pulling this man through the rushes took all Bob's remaining strength. Bob dropped him down next to Bruce and saw, for the first time, his identity. It was Ed.

CHAPTER 15

***

"Ed....you okay?" was all Bob, surprised, could say.

He should have known the man he hauled out of the water was Ed. He and Bruce hunted together often. He especially should have figured it out based on Ed's size. Everything had all happened so fast. The storm blew in fast. Duke ran into trouble almost immediately, and he didn't have a whole lot of time to sit and think when he saw the two hunters in trouble.

"I'm cold. Where's Bruce?" Ed said, trying to sit up and locate his hunting partner.

"He's right here," Bob point said, pointing toward the lifeless body laying only six feet away.

"I'm going to try to get a fire going," Bob

continued, and stooped to check on Bruce.

He was breathing, but not responsive at all. Duke lay next to him, head up, but shivering.

Bob liked to be prepared. You had to be if you chose to hunt alone from time to time. Now, however, he wished Al or Cliff were with him. He had two guys to get warmed up, plus his dog. Duke was shivering, that was probably a good sign. Bruce was a concern, but right now he had to find some dry wood to get a fire going. He had a plastic container, the same kind he kept lead jig heads in for walleye fishing, full of matches. He checked his pants pocket and found that the plastic cylinder was still there. He always kept that cylinder with him when he was fishing or hunting. A lesson he learned when he dumped his canoe fishing once on a cold October morning. He had wished he had matches to start a warm fire then.

As Ed and Duke silently watched, Bob scrambled about on the edge of the woods grabbing any wood he could find, some small branches for kindling and some larger logs from downed trees. However, everything he found was wet, or covered with a layer of ice or snow. Quickly, Bob snapped some small branches, kicked clear the 3 or 4 inches of snow that had quickly accumulated just inside the tree line, a bit out of the wind, and tried to light them. He couldn't get the damp sticks to catch a flame. He tried again, adjusting his crouch, trying to block the wind.

"Too damn wet," he said aloud.

He quickly pulled out his pocket knife and looked around. Through the snow, he saw what he was looking for, an old dead elm tree, uprooted and rotting. Bob grabbed a strong hold on a piece of bark and pulled. The bark pulled free fairly easily, exposing the soft, dry inner layer of the tree. With his jackknife he scraped some of the crumbly, rotting wood into his cold hands. A couple spoonfuls in his hand, and he hurriedly put them down in his cleared spot, blocking the wind again. He put a match to it. It caught a flame right away, but as soon as Bob threw some kindling on top, the damp sticks wouldn't catch, and his fire burned out. He quickly scraped some more wood, getting a bigger handful this time.

"Got a fire going yet?" Ed hollered through the wind.

"Working on it, everything's so wet." Bob yelled back.

"Gas!" Ed yelled.

"What?!" Bob paused, looking at the big man

lying in the snow.

"You got gas in your motor!" Ed said, trying to get up. "Not sure how'll you get it out though."

With Ed watching, Bob jumped into this boat. He grabbed his shotgun that was still there. With all the excitement in the past 30 minutes, he had forgotten about his 12 gauge. The Winchester Model 12 his father had given him was sitting half in and half out of the water in his boat. He quickly unscrewed the barrel from the rest of his shotgun. He could use it to siphon the gas out of the motor. As he began taking the gas cap off the top of his Evinrude, he paused. Where would he put the gas?

Sitting up from the rear bench seat of his boat, he opened the top wooden cover to his storage box. He pulled out a plastic bag containing a roll of toilet paper. He never left for a day of hunting or fishing without his knife, his matches, and of course, his roll of toilet paper. Bob dumped out his metal shell box, about a foot across, four inches wide, and six inches deep and used to hold his shotgun shells. He put the dry toilet paper inside. Working at his father's garage, Bob had siphoned gas many times. He knew just how hard to suck on the hose to get the fuel moving. Using a shotgun barrel in place of a hose should work.

After removing the gas cap, he lowered the barrel into the gas tank, housed inside his 16 horse Evinrude. Once the gas rose inside the barrel he quickly pulled it out and released the fuel into the shell box and on top of the toilet paper. One more barrel full of gas on top of the fuel soaked toilet paper, he slammed the shell box cover shut and bounded from the boat. He'd get a fire going now.

My grandfather, Nic Steffes.

CHAPTER 16

***

When Nic Steffes got out of bed very early on Monday morning, November 11th, he was eager to get some work done. Buzz, as usual, would be working with him. His work had piled up, even though it was a holiday. He needed Bob to lend him a hand at his garage. If they worked hard and were able to catch up on the workload, he'd take his son duck hunting. The day looked like another warm one, not unlike the recent trend of unseasonably warm, sunny days they had been experiencing lately. He figured it was a fair exchange for some hard work.

As he drove his '34 Ford the mile or so with Buzz and Bob. All his youngest son could talk about was duck hunting. The kid could hunt and fish every day if he let him.

His 16 year old son was a fine young man, not as grounded as his 21 year old, Charles, but certainly a hardworking, motivated individual. The problem was, Bob wasn't too focused on school. He was a motivated athlete and outdoorsman, but Nic wished he would make some decisions about what he wanted to do to earn a living. His son was smart enough to get a college degree. But Nic knew any job requiring his son to sit at a desk wasn't going to work for Bob. He needed to be outdoors. He would have tried convincing Bob to wait it out, work in the garage, and eventually begin taking over. But, Charles, or Buzz as he nicknamed his oldest son, had already declared his interest in that game plan. Besides, Buzz was an exceptional mechanic, probably as good as he was, and willing to put in the long hours Nic thought necessary to cater to the people of Winona. Hopefully, Bob would decide to pursue a job with the Corp. of Engineers working on the river. He was a strong young man, didn't mind the physical aspects of a job, and loved the river. It would be a perfect situation for him.

The three men worked through the morning,

struggling to keep up. Whenever they thought they were getting ahead, someone would drop off their car, keeping the log jam of vehicles needing repair going. It was a typical Monday for the trusted mechanic.

By late morning, Nic knew he wasn't going to make it out in the duck blind.
Besides it was a bluebird day, temperature in the mid-fifties and a sunny sky. Too nice for duck hunting. Nic preferred a little wind and rain to keep the birds moving and flying low. But he knew that didn't matter to his son Bob. That kid would hunt even when the hunting was no good.

By 10:30 A.M., Nic decided to send Bob home. He trusted his son to go out alone with the boat and hunt until dark. Knowing his son, the kid would probably bring his fishing rod along to kill the time, waiting for flocks of ducks that seemed to be stuck up north, enjoying the nice weather.

CHAPTER 17

***

Bob helped the shivering Ed move closer to the fire, just starting to take off. As soon as the match had hit the gasoline soaked roll of toilet paper, the flames increased quickly, strong enough to dry and catch the twigs and sticks added to the white ball of flames. Ed was able to add wood as Bob began hauling Bruce, still motionless, to the warmth. Duke managed to struggle to his feet, shivering violently, but able to follow his master carrying Bruce.

"Ed, try to get Bruce warm and revived. I'll be back," Bob said through the wind and went back to his boat, hopped in, and dug into his boat seat storage box. He blew on his hands as he touched the cold metal of his boat seat, and pulled out his plastic bag with his extra clothes.

Just as he slammed the seat shut, he heard another boat motor faintly through the roar of the wind. By now, Bob could only see 20 yards out into the lake. He strained to hear the motor, trying to judge how far out it was. He rubbed his chilled face as the wind and snow slammed into him. Shaking his head, he could only hope that whoever it was, they would make it. The waves were still rolling, probably higher than before, and his boat was again half filled with water, taking it on from the back end like it had earlier. They would have to be on their own. He gave a shout into the wind, a loud "Hey! Over here!" But he knew that they couldn't hear him. He gave a thought to the idea that maybe it was someone coming out to look for him, or for Bruce and Ed. Yet, from the sound of the boat motor, they were heading toward the mouth of Twin Lakes, trying to make it home. He wrapped his arms around his plastic bag, jumped out of the boat and headed for the fire.

Bob came in past the fire, where Ed was now sitting on the ground, holding Bruce. Duke was acting funny. He had his tail between his legs, still shivering, and was sniffing Bruce around the face.

Bob began unrolling the big plastic bag, "I have a sweatshirt in my dry bag. Let's quick get his jacket and shirt off. We can put it on Bruce. Maybe a dry shirt and a good fire will help him out."

"Don't worry about it," Ed said flatly.

"No, it's okay, I've warmed up from all the rowing. Bruce needs it more than you or I," Bob continued, leaning in to hand the sweatshirt to Ed.

"He's dead," Ed interrupted.

Bob stopped his motion, the shock of the news leaving him not sure what to say, what to do. Silence took hold.

After a moment, Bob stood up, his eyes blinking into the snow filled wind, "You sure? I mean, we can try to warm him up some, maybe...."

"No use, I checked on him while you were down to your boat. He's done for," Ed replied just loud enough to be heard in the wind.

"I'm sorry," Bob said, "but that doesn't have to be us."

"I'm froze, you hear?!" Ed yelled, anger rising in his voice.

"We have a fire, we can stay warm!" Bob yelled back.

Ed sat up from the log he was leaning against, "Bruce was by the fire, but it's not enough, he still died!"

"Well, I don't plan on dyin'! Get up and start moving, or you will freeze to death!" Bob yelled and stepped around the dying fire and pulled on Ed's arms trying to get him up.

"My feet are froze! I can't stand up!" Ed protested.

Bob let go of the big man and grabbed some branches from a tree, snapped them off, and threw them in the small fire. He then helped Ed get closer to the fire and began pulling off Ed's hip boots, stopping every few seconds to blow on his cold hands. The wool socks on Ed's feet were wet and as cold as ice. Bob struggled to pull them off. Looking up, he squinted against the snow and wind but saw some low hanging branches that he could hang the frozen socks for now, then began rubbing Ed's feet firmly, trying to bring some feeling back.

In a couple minutes, with Ed keeping his feet as close to the fire as he dared, he started to wince in pain as the feeling began coming back into his lower limbs.

Darkness had settled into the river bottoms as hunters hunkered down, preparing to brave a cold night in a blizzard that many never saw coming.

CHAPTER 18

***

Bad weather was a part of living in Minnesota. Those who grew up there had become accustomed to snow storms, ice storms, or hard rains that filled the little creeks that fed the Mississippi River to capacity, flooding valleys and parts of town. When bad weather came, most people sat inside, waiting by their radio, gathered in silence in their living room, waiting for the weather updates.

Yet growing up in the Mississippi River valley often meant that the men of the community were fishing or hunting at certain times of the year. These outdoorsman, territorial about their space as they are, never failed to look out for one another. In times of need, whether it was helping another fisherman with a tow in when their boat motor failed, or assisting a hunter on a blood trail, everyone knew that they too, would need a hand to bail them out of a sticky situation at some stage. On November 11th, 1940, the men of Winona, Minnesota gathered at Swedes Bar to determine a way to help the hunters stranded in the river bottoms in what was becoming a storm of unprecedented proportions.

Families of hunters and those who made it to safety earlier, were now exchanging information at Swedes . The crowd listened intently as hunters coming in from the marshes reported who they may have seen that morning, or whose truck they knew was still parked at the various boat landings leading to the maze of sloughs and backwater channels.

Many people had attended the concert at St. Teresa's University that evening where Walter Liberace from West Allis, Wisconsin had played his piano. Liberace had wrapped up his performance by playing "The Night Winds", an irony that did not go unnoticed by the large crowd in the auditorium.

CHAPTER 19

***

By nightfall, both men were finally getting beyond the point where they feared they would meet Bruce's fate. Bob had spent nearly two hours frantically gathering wood for the fire, which had to be kept high. Bob wanted the blaze to dry off their coats, still hung on saplings near enough to the fire to warm. He would carry or drag as much timber as he could to the fire, throw it in a pile, and trudge off through the snow to find more. Each time, Bob would pause to check on Ed, who had managed to pull a log closer to the fire for a seat. Even Duke was looking better. He had managed to scratch a clear spot in the snow near the fire, close to Ed, trying to keep warm. Staying dry was like fighting a losing battle. The snow was still screaming in from the northwest, soaking the men as quickly as the fire could dry them. Thankfully the strip of land they were on was high enough to keep the ground they were on dry. The waves out in the lake had steadily grown higher after nightfall and were now crashing well into the woods where the men were trying to dry out by their fire.

Bob was no longer worried about Ed, when he saw him get up from the fire, walk into the woods, and begin searching for wood. The search was difficult due to the rain and ice that arrived before the snow. All exposed downed timber was frozen solid, nearly impossible to pull free from the ground. They had to work hard to climb under windfalls in the snow to find wood, kept dry by the debris above.

They were on an island, a peninsula really, connected to a long, island strip, probably a half mile long at least. Where they were, at the point of the attached peninsula, it was less than 50 yards wide, arching around the bay, Bob called his own hunting and fishing spot, then connecting to the island. The island ran like many in the river valley, parallel to the flow of the river and line of bluffs on either side. This particular strip of island separated the Minnesota City river bottoms from Pap Slough, just one narrow waterway from the main channel of the Mississippi River. Even though the peninsula they were on was relatively narrow, Bob was careful not to stray too far from the fire. The driving snow and low visibility played games with his bearings, forcing him, while looking for wood, to often locate the water's edge and work his way back to the fire. He was constantly getting turned around in the dense cover of buck brush and saplings, confused in the blowing snow. He soon realized that by paying attention to which direction the wind was blowing as he left the fire in search of wood, he could find his way back by using the wind's direction to point the way.

"Bob, give me a hand with this log!" came Ed's shout through the wind.

It was the first time Ed had spoken since earlier in the day. Bob had kept his distance, allowing the man to come to grips with the death of his friend. Bob considered Bruce to be a decent guy. Like Ed, he was two years older than Bob, and a former high school baseball teammate. Sure they competed against one another often, but he always seemed like a mild mannered guy who liked the same things Bob did, hunting and playing some baseball. Bob had kept busy getting firewood for more reasons than just keeping alive. He was uncomfortable being around Ed, especially when the big man seemed in such an emotionally fragile state.

Bob located Ed in the snow, still penetrating the woods. Ed had found an old dead tree that had been uprooted, probably in an earlier storm. In the early evening darkness, it looked pretty rotten. Vegetation had grown over the top and the snow concealed it well.

"Fell over it in the snow!" Ed shouted through the wind. "It's pretty rotten, but the weeds have grown over it....kept it pretty dry."

Bob began kicking snow, now over six inches deep, away from the big tree, its outline barely visible in the grass and snow.

Both men grabbed an end and pulled it free from the ice, snow, and vegetation. The tree was big for one found on a narrow peninsula in the river bottoms, as big in diameter as a bucket. The spring floods usually overtook these type of islands, keeping the ground soft nearly all year round. Big trees usually succumbed to their own mass, toppling over, their roots finding only mud and water to hang onto. Wind storms usually took a toll on them in the river bottoms, knocking them down; their root systems exposed in a muddy hole. It was these fallen trees that Bob, and now Ed, were finding and adding to their pile to more than likely, get them through the night. Stumbling as they went, they picked their way through the snowstorm and the dense forest to their campfire, now beginning to burn down.

"Plop your end down on the flames," Ed said, breathing heavy from the exertion.

It was clear that Ed was still feeling the effects of his icy plunge as he himself plopped down on his log by the flames. He again rested his head in his hands.

"I'll get the flames back up," Bob said and shoved some smaller kindling under the big log.

Ed didn't say anything. Bob sensed that fatigue and sadness over the loss of his friend were hitting Ed hard.

"You know, we're not going home tonight....no way. The waves are still way too high, and my boat is half filled with water. We need to get a shelter going, get our clothes dry, or we're in for a really long night," Bob said, feeling the coats and t-shirts hanging on the bent branches of the saplings.

Looking up, Ed nodded in agreement.

"If you can make it, we can drag my boat up here into the woods, we can prop it up somehow, use it for shelter.

"I can make it," Ed said, rising to his feet.

Both men made their way down to the water and together, dragged the boat out as far as they could, like Bob had done earlier in the day. Pushing hard, they tipped it on its side to drain.

CHAPTER 20

***

It was midafternoon Monday, November 11th, Armistice Day, and Max Conrad had just stepped out of his airplane hangar to get some cool air. The warm, damp fall air had made his hangar too warm. Even though it was a holiday, Max was taking advantage of the wonderful weather to get some work done.

The fall had been unseasonably warm thus far, and today was no different, cloudy with a temperature in the 50's, and a light drizzle moving in, taking over the blue skies that had been prevalent earlier in the day.

Max Conrad owned and operated a small aircraft flight school at the little Winona airport. Somewhat of a pioneer in operating small aircraft, Max gave flying lessons out of his hangar.

One of his flying students had cancelled this morning to go duck hunting, although the hunters in town had been grumbling that the ducks were taking their time working their way down from their northern nesting areas in Canada and the Dakotas.

Max himself wasn't a duck hunter, a minority in town, but he recognized the beauty of the area the hunters explored, having flown his planes over the many backwater sloughs and chains of islands that lined the main channel of the Mississippi River.

Max went about his business working on the new ceiling in his Winona hangar. Outside, shortly after noon, the wind shifted, bringing some much needed cool air to the area. Soon after that, by 3:00 P.M., the light drizzle turned to rain, and the rain turned to sleet as the temperature dropped rapidly.

The pilot decided to head home for the day. The winds had picked up, rattling the sides of the hangar, and the cloud ceiling had dropped. There would be no flying today. Besides, he had promised to take his wife Betty to a piano concert at St. Theresa's College that evening, and he would need to clean up from his ceiling work at his hangar.

After dinner, Max and Betty drove through the snow, now beginning to pile up on the city streets to St. Theresa's auditorium and joined the large crowd beginning to take their seats. The buzz in the crowd was, of course, about the storm, the big change in temperature, and about those they knew out duck hunting, and hoping everyone would make it back safely after the sunset shoot, the best time for good shooting, just at dusk.

Max, too, was hoping everyone was staying safe. From years of flying over the marshes and maze of backwater on the Minnesota side of the river, the Winona airport was located next to some of these waterways. His takeoffs took him over them daily, so he knew navigating them in blinding snow could be treacherous. Being a pilot, he also knew the wind. Even in the sloughs, away from the main channel of the Mississippi River, Max knew that the water would be rough and hunters would be running the risk of capsizing their boats or hitting logs as they attempted to get back to the boat landings.

The discussion of the crowd subsided as the curtain drew open and out stepped Walter Liberace, an up and coming concert pianist.

Like others in the sold out auditorium, Max and Betty were enthralled by the performance Walter Liberace gave that night, even though at times the roar of the wind outside could be heard in the auditorium and threatened to overtake the sounds of Liberace's piano and end the concert early. Several times during the concert, the young musician stopped playing and appeared to be relinquishing to the whistling winds heard loudly inside and interrupting his music, but he continued on.

When Liberace finished his performance, he took a couple of bows and began to leave the stage. An ongoing thunderous applause prompted the young man to return for an encore. Two more encores followed and the night ended when he played the song, "The Night Winds", an eerie reminder of the events unfolding just outside the auditorium doors.

Liberace ended his song, came to the front of the stage, thanked the crowd, and threatened never to come back, recognizing the harsh conditions outside.

CHAPTER 21

***

Nic and Buzz had finally started to put a dent in their workload by early afternoon. Their garage doors had been open most of the day, and they were surprised when a light rain began to fall, accompanied by a sudden drop in temperature.

By 4:00, the rain had turned to snow and the wind picked up. Shortly after that, the phone rang, and Nic left the garage bay and slipped into the little office to answer.

Buzz had just walked outside with a customer, only to be greeted by a brisk wind. The first snowflakes began to fall, coming in sideways in the gale. He shook his head and gave his father a worried grimace when he entered the office to find his father on the phone.

Nic was trying to reassure his wife over the phone, "Buzz and I will drive over to Vercota Landing; I'm sure with all the hunters coming in at the same time, the boat landing is pretty congested...a lineup of guys waiting to trailer their boats."

"It's pretty nasty out Dad," Buzz said shaking his head. "I bet the temperature has dropped 15, 20 degrees since we arrived this morning."

"Let's take a drive over to Vercota," Nic said to his son as he gazed into the snowstorm from just inside his garage door. "Nobody will be stopping by anymore today."

They finished up the work on the last car hastily, and Nic followed Buzz as he drove the car to the owner's house.

"Wow, who would have guessed we'd see snow today after how warm it was this morning," Buzz said, as he and his father climbed into their car.

"Yeah, let's hope your little brother had enough sense to head for home by now," Nic told his oldest son still trying to send some reassurance his way.

Nic tried to hurry down Mercer Street, until they reached the old highway that led them upriver to run parallel to the river. The grain bins perched on the banks of the river were barely visible through the driving snow. Nic didn't want to appear nervous, but his truck fish-tailed on the now six inches of snow often as they drove, and Nic knew Buzz could tell he was worried. The wind along the river was even stronger than in town, and even in the white haze of wind and snow, big white caps could be seen on the water.

"Good Lord," Buzz murmured from the passenger's seat.

"Yeah, those look to be three footers out there," Nic replied. "I'm sure your brother is cussin' the wind, probably sitting at the dock at Vercota waiting his turn to bring the boat in.

"Hope you're right," Buzz said flatly.

As they continued along the road, now going past back water sloughs, marshes, and bottomland, the main channel having shifted to the Wisconsin side, they passed only a couple other vehicles.

After darkness enveloped the river valley, and waiting by the boat landing for over an hour, Nic and Buzz realized that with the temperatures dropping to near zero after starting the day at nearly 60 degrees, they'd better head back while they could. Several vehicles with trailers were still in the parking lot, including the Steffes's truck.

Only one pair of hunters made it to the boat landing while Nic and his son Buzz waited in their truck.

"Everybody okay?" Nic shouted through the wind when he approached the cold, wet hunters in the dark.

"Yeah, but we need to get somewhere warm and dry," The hunter replied with a chuckle as he crawled out of his boat, the other hunter busy knocking the ice off his motor, so he could shut it off.

"We're looking for my son!" Nic shouted, stooping on the dock to hold the boat steady while Buzz helped the other man, soaking wet and shivering, out of his boat. "You guys see a single hunter out there, 16 years old?"

"No!" the shivering hunter responded. "But, you can't see much of anything out there. The snow's blowing in sideways!"

"Where abouts were you guys?" Bob continued to press the hunter for information.

"We were down river from here, out along the southern end of Crooked Slough," the man said, and watched as his buddy was attempting to back the truck and trailer down to the water through the snow drifts. The deep snow was now threatening to make the slope of the boat landing impossible to navigate.

"Yeah, I think my son was heading up river, out onto Twin Lakes," Bob continued to shout through the wind.

"Well, your son is probably hunkered down on an island waiting it out," the hunter told Nic, sensing the concern in his voice.

"Thanks! You're probably right. We'll give you a hand getting up the ramp. Then we should all get out of here before we get stranded at the ramp in these drifts," Nic yelled through the wind.

Nic and Buzz helped the hunters, frozen and moving stiffly, load their boat on the trailer and then push the truck, boat and trailer in tow, up the ramp, the hunter's truck tires spinning in the deep snow, searching for a footing to get up the incline and back onto the road back into town.

"He'll be fine," Buzz tried to reassure his father as Nic maneuvered his truck around drifts and fought to keep it on the road back toward Winona.

"Yeah, he's always been prepared while hunting. He'll have extra clothes and knows enough to hunker down and wait it out," Nic replied, trying to talk himself into believing his youngest son would be okay on such a night alone in the Mississippi backwaters.

On their way back home, they swung into Swedes Bar to check on word from anybody who made it back from the river.

Nic and Buzz parked the truck where they could outside the old tavern and fought their way inside, pulling up their jacket collars against the 40 mile an hour winds whipping down Center Street off the river. Surprisingly they found a big crowd inside, all coming inside for the same purpose, seeking information about their loved ones.

"Over here," Buzz said to his father, and lead the way through groups of worried people to Tom Baab and Dave Tadewald, from the McGuire's baseball team.

"Hey," Tom said when he saw Buzz, taking a moment to shake hands with Bob's brother. "Bob?"

"No," Nic said, coming forward to shake hands with his son's friends and teammates. "His truck is still at Vercota."

"We waited for over an hour, but only one set of hunters came in," Buzz added. "He must be waiting it out."

"I'm sure that's what he's doing, Mr. Steffes,"

Tom said reassuringly. "I've hunted with him. He's probably got a cooler full of sandwiches, sharing his meal with Duke, sittin' by a fire right now."

"You're probably right," Nic said.

"Guys over at the end of the bar are talking about going out first thing in the morning to find friends of theirs," Dave said, pointing to a couple guys talking to Swede Gordon, the bar owner.

"Yeah, if you need help tomorrow, let us know," Tom offered.

"I will," Nic replied. "Thanks guys."

As Nic and Buzz sat in the warm bar, having a drink and discussing their options for first thing in the morning, more people arrived, including some men who had spoken to Stanley Duncanson, the Winona Police Captain. Plans were being made to bring home those who at that very moment were fighting for their lives.

CHAPTER 22

***

It was the beginning of a long night for Ed and Bob. With a lot of work they were able to drag the boat, having to turn it on its side several times to get it through the trees to the fire. They managed to prop it up with a log, leaving enough room to squeeze underneath. Right away they were pleased at how effective the shelter was at keeping the wind off them. The unbelievably rapid drop in temperature pushed the young men to work hard to keep the fire going.

"We need to move that fire underneath the boat, or we'll lose it," Ed said as both men sat hunched over underneath the boat as the wind whipped around the fire, positioned just outside the perimeter of the upside down aluminum craft.

"Yeah, how can we move it?" shouted Bob through the wind still penetrating their little shelter.

Without answering, Ed climbed out from underneath the boat, and using his gloved hands, feet, and the end of a log, pushed and slid the little fire underneath their boat.

"That'll help!" Bob said as Ed began feeding the wood they had collected in to Bob, who stacked it in a pile underneath their shelter.

"That should keep us going for a while," Ed said as he crawled back under the boat. "If we lose the fire, we're done for. It'll be a bit smoky in here, but at least we'll stay warm."

"Good idea," Bob said, squinting as the wind pushed the smoke from the fire into their shelter.

Bob could tell that Ed was feeling better, starting to warm up. His actions tending to the fire and straightening up the small area under the boat, to get comfortable for a long night, was a good sign that the big man was recovering from his near tragic experience just hours earlier.

Bob had divided up the extra clothes from his dry bag. Ed took the sweatshirt and stocking hat, while Bob had put the dry sweatpants on underneath his hunting pants that were wet but beginning to dry as they sat near the fire. Bob's hands had been very painful for hours. His gloves had become soaked while rowing his boat out to retrieve Duke, then Bruce and Ed. The dry gloves from his little bag were a welcome relief.

While Bob had been busy earlier hauling his gear underneath the boat, his gun, shell box, dry bag, and decoy bag, he tried not to stare as Ed had gingerly picked up the body of his friend and carefully place Bruce on the back side of the boat, opposite the side they propped up. Knowing that Bruce was just on the other side of the aluminum boat wall as he tried to hunker down to wait out the storm was a bit unnerving, but they didn't know what else to do with the body. Hopefully, they would find a way to get back to the boat landing tomorrow, and come back for Bruce later.

The men tried to cushion the ground under the boat with some branches and long grasses they pulled from under the snow. Their clothing had not completely dried, and their chill was constant. It was 10:00 P.M. now, and both men were settling in, glad to be out of the wind at least. The ground was still cold, especially when the heat of their bodies and the fire melted some of the remaining snow underneath them, and then cooled off when the fire died down. Duke was restless, trying to curl tightly against Bob. The dog's shivering kept Bob from sleeping too much.

Both men worried about the fire going out. Their fear prevented them from sleeping too deeply. Around midnight, they were forced to venture out in the howling wind and darkness to find more wood. They both knew that if the wood ran out, it may spell the end for them.

Even with their attempts to dry their clothing, the dampness was unbearable, and forced them to flip over often as they lay under the boat, trying to keep both sides of their body warm and dry.

With the howling wind, the crackling of the fire, and the snow blowing into their shelter, and with their attempts to create a dry environment in which to spend the night, both men managed to fall asleep again after midnight. Duke snuggled in tight to his owner, covered up with the empty decoy bag.

Their sleep was interrupted only a couple hours later when Ed woke with a start, "Bob! Bob! Hey! Wake up!"

Bob woke and in the low firelight saw Ed sitting up under the boat digging underneath the tree branches he was using as a bed.

"I got a bunch of water coming in under the boat!" yelled Ed over the howling wind.

Both men crawled out from under the boat and were greeted with water pushing through the woods, colliding with their upside down boat, then retreating.

"The waves must be huge on the lake!" Bob shouted. "They're overtaking our spot."

"Shoot! Let's move the boat!" Ed yelled back in the wind, "Grab a burning log out of the fire before the water gets it!"

Bob turned on his flashlight as Ed cautiously tried to pull a still burning branch from the fire, trying to salvage their warmth. The wind and snow whipped the flames on the branch Ed picked from what was left from the fire, threatening to extinguish the flame from the three inch diameter stick as soon as it was picked from the fire. Sparks flew off the stick in the wind as Bob, standing in the surging waters, coming and going in wind drawn waves, shined his light farther back into the aspens.

Ed tried to shelter the fading flame from the wind with his body. Then upon seeing their fire being engulfed in flowing water, stuck the stick under the cover of the upturned boat in an attempt to keep a flame.

"Bob, I'm losing the flame!" Ed yelled and looking up, pinpointed the younger man's light, flickering amongst the trees and blinding snow, just within sight, yet only 15 feet away. The flashlight approached and Bob came back into view.

"Our strip of land is too narrow, and too low!" Bob said coming around the boat and quickly reaching into the fading fire to pull out a bigger, mostly burned chunk of wood. He quickly dropped it onto the bottom of the of overturned boat to avoid burning his hands.

"We need to save the fire!" Bob yelled, looking around for an answer in the darkness and snow.

"I know!" Ed hollered back. "What can we…?"

"The shell box!" Bob interrupted, diving underneath the boat and pulling out the metal shell box, now empty.

"Bust off the stick and put the hot end in here! Should be a little gas still on the bottom" Bob yelled. "No! No! Wait!" Bob yelled again, pulling the shell box away from Ed and reached back under the boat, coming back out into the wind again with a handful of sticks from the collection they accumulated under their aluminum shelter.

"Okay, try it now," Bob said, standing tight against Ed to block the wind.

Ed snapped off the smoldering end of his stick

and dropped it in the shell box a split second before Bob followed up with a handful of sticks. The sticks smoked in the metal box, but no flame caught hold.

"Damn!" Bob shouted, as both men peered into the shell box hoping for a flame.

Bob handed the shell box to Ed, and quickly dug into his damp hunting pants to reveal a small lock blade knife. Immediately he reached under his shirt with the blade and with a couple quick arm motions, pulled out a piece of shirt.

"Here! Try to soak up any gas left inside with this," Bob said, still huddled close to Ed, both men working together to save their fire, as water rushed over their strip of land and woods from the huge waves on Twin Lakes, now over four feet high and being pushed from the vicious, biting north wind.

Ed dug his hand around the bottom of the shell box. "I can smell gas!" Ed exclaimed. "Light!" he yelled, pleading for a flame.

Bob, again using his knife, grabbed the log and attempted to hack off the smoldering parts and hit the little shell box in the darkness and wind. Ed immediately began to lightly blow in the metal box, doing all he could to entice a flame.

"Yes!" Ed exclaimed a moment later as a flame

took off on the bottom of the box and began to take hold of the other kindling inside.

CHAPTER 23

***

It was after midnight when Nic and Buzz were able to make it home from Swedes. It was hard to tell just how much snow there was on the ground. Drifts were forming everywhere, and with all the wind, it was impossible to tell how much of the white stuff they had.

"I bet we got a good foot out there," Buzz said as he and his father came in the house, brushing the snow off their coats.

Ellen came into the kitchen with Esther, both in robes, and red swollen eyes.

Ellen tried to say something to her husband, but quickly burst into tears, embracing her husband, sobbing into his snow covered coat.

"Ellen, Bob will be just fine," Nic said, trying his best to reassure his wife.

"Mom, the kid's tougher than he looks," Buzz backed his father, trying to lighten the mood with some kidding around.

"Here, sit down," Nic said to his wife and helped the shaken woman into a chair.

With Esther and Buzz joining them at the table, Nic explained what the plan was.

"There were a lot of guys at Swedes Bar. Several had talked to Stanley Duncanson. Sounds like he's already called the Corp. of Engineers asking for their help. Someone said they were going to call Max Conrad and see if he can get his plane up to look for hunters first thing in the morning." Nic filled in his wife.

Esther sat in tears, her head in her hands, as Ellen, still sobbing, nodded her head as she took in her husband's information.

"What can we do?" Ellen managed to say through the tears.

"Right now…a few prayers and some sleep. "I'll call Stanley first thing in the morning and see what we can do to help the search. "I guarantee Stan will be working all night long on setting up some sort of search starting at first light. There's not much we can do tonight," Nic continued.

"Don't worry. Bob is probably hunkered down in his boat, waiting it out. He'll be just fine," Nic tried to reassure his family.

He hoped he was right.

CHAPTER 24

***

At 3:45 A.M., the men made the decision that to stay dry, they would need to walk the narrow island down river toward the mouth of Twin Lakes, in search of a higher piece of land to hole up for the night or find some help.

"Wait!" Ed yelled through the wind as they began to work their way through the trees, water invading their woods with each rolling wave. In the dark, Bob could see Ed, lifting Bruce's lifeless body and placing it on top of the overturned boat. He stepped back toward Bob for a moment, water sloshing up to his ankles, then ducked back under the boat, and even in the darkness, he could see Ed pull out Bob's model 12. "Okay, let's go," Ed said and pointed downriver, handing Bob his prized shotgun signaling him to begin the hike.

Their distance covered was unknown in the darkness, snow, and dense cover of the 50 foot wide strip of land. The going was tough. Deep snow and a hidden tangle of brush, fallen trees, and vines grabbed at their feet as they trudged through the blizzard. Bob lead the way, shotgun in one hand, constantly searching for a penetrable route with the flashlight in his other hand. Ed followed with the shell box, smoke trickling from the slightly open lid, immediately whisked away in the wind.

Bob had stopped to catch his breath and gain his bearings when he felt Ed's hand on his shoulder. "Hey, I think the wind is letting up."

Bob rotated his head, ducking under some branches the best he could in the dark, and noticed for the first time, the wind was in fact dying down.

"Luckily," Bob said over his shoulder, "Cuz it sure isn't getting any warmer."

Both men paused now, taking a break from pushing aside small trees and sloshing through a combination of heavy snow and slushy water as the low sitting island continued to be overrun by the waves of Twin Lakes on their right.

To the left was another channel, Pap Slough, that paralleled the island they were on now. The channel was only about 150 yards wide at its widest. Across the channel was one more strip of wooded land, broken up by sand bars created by high water on the Mississippi, just to the other side. Bob could see that channel through the trees, and could see that the waves had calmed down, with only a few white caps breaking in the dark.

As the front moved through, the temperature had dropped into the teens and was still dropping. Ed stopped occasionally to add kindling to their small fire, smoldering safely in the metal shell box. Duke was glad to be moving again, nimbly working his way through the dense saplings and larger downed trees. Bob used Duke's lead to pick the most navigable path.

It was about an hour before dawn when both men came to the mouth of Twin Lakes, where Pickerel Run entered. The snow was quickly letting up along with the wind, the air becoming cold and crisp with over a foot of snow.

As Bob was slogging his way to the point of the long, narrow strip of land running along the side of Twin Lake, he suddenly stopped.

"What?" Ed said, nearly bumping into Bob.

"What's this all about?" Bob said, looking at his feet and shining his flashlight at an area around a tree, a ring of packed snow.

Ed came alongside Bob, peering at the ground as well. "Looks like someone was here, those are boot tracks."

"Yeah, was someone walking circles all night?" Bob questioned, beginning to shine his light in the woods near the big tree with encircling boot tracks.

"Wait, shine your light over there," Ed said grabbing Bob's arm and guiding his aim to a small windfall only 15 feet away where Duke was now nosing around.

Tracks could be seen in the snow leading right to the windfall. Bob's light hit a dark mass under the branches where two trees had fallen together, crisscrossing each other on their way down. Bob made his way over to the windfall with Ed in tow; Duke bounced around both sides of the downed trees. Before they made it to the windfall, they already knew what was underneath. Two hunters, huddled together under the branches, much like Bob and Ed had done earlier under the boat, lay on the ground motionless. Ed reached under the branches and touched the men, both probably in their 50's, their shotguns leaning against some bigger branches. There was no response to Ed's touch.

Ed shook his head, "Froze. Let's keep going. They must have walked in circles all night, trying to stay warm."

"The end of this chunk of land is right here," Bob said, quickening his pace to the end of the wooded strip of land they were on.

What was left of his light shone across the mouth of Twin Lakes. The big, dead elm that had marked the end of Bob's canoe race so many times before was just across the water. Twin Lakes, widened to their right and Pickerel Run flowed past on their left, diverging into the lake. Ice was starting to form along the edges of the point of land, already reaching 20 yards into the lake in the now, much calmer water.

"Okay...now what?" Ed asked looking at cold water ahead of them, with no way of getting to the next island over.

"Hmm, I don't know," Bob said with a grimace.

"What do you mean you don't know!" Ed shouted. "I thought you had a plan to get us off this snow covered, never ending chunk of land!"

"I never said that!" Bob yelled back.

"Well, hell! If I knew you'd lead us to a dead end, I'd never have followed you!" Ed continued yelling, his big voice booming in the cold air, his arms raised in disgust.

"You didn't have to follow! We couldn't have stayed with the boat, the whole place was being flooded by the waves pouring into the woods," Bob said back, trying to control his anger. "I was hoping we could make it to the point and find some other guys, waiting out the storm…or flag down a boat coming through Pickerel Run."

"Well, that plan ain't gonna work! Pickerel Run is froze over and I don't see a lineup of guys waiting to lend us a hand!" Ed said, jabbing his finger in Bob's chest menacingly.

The whole scenario reminded Bob too much of his summer run-in with Ed. His breathing was rapid, his emotions racing from anger to fear and back again. Bob slapped Ed's gloved hand away from his chest and shoved the big man. Ed was barely rocked off balance and like the night at the Chimney, grabbed Bob by the front of his coat, slamming him against a tree. Bob's attempts to free himself from Ed's strong grasp went nowhere. Even in the dark, Bob could see the anger in Ed's face. His anger was interrupted by Duke's angry bark and throaty growl as the black lab came forward, the fur bristled on his back, ready to defend his master.

Then, the anger in the big man began to recede. He let go of Bob, slowly releasing his grip. Both men stood, face to face, as the first glimpse of dawn could be seen in the east, across Pickerel Run. Ed looked down at the dog and his tension eased.

Ed took a couple steps away from Bob, "Settle down pup," Ed said calmly, "Everything's fine....I just need to think."

Ed sat down in the snow, again putting his head in his hands.

"Sorry about Bruce," Bob said finally.

"No. I'm sorry. You risked your life to save mine. I knew where this piece of land went. It's not the first time I've duck hunted out here. Guess I just figured you knew a spot we could cross somewhere, keep going, and get to Minnesota City somehow," Ed said, rubbing his hands on his cold face.

"Well, maybe..." Bob began, looking across the partially frozen mouth of Twin Lakes, then across Pickerel Run, a gentle flowing slough 50 yards wide, now nearly all ice covered.

"No way, I know what you're thinkin'. That ice is too thin. Hell, that was open water less than

12 hours ago." Ed interrupted.

"You're right," Bob said, exasperated. "But, if we wait here, we'll end up like those guys over there," Bob said pointing in the direction of the two frozen hunters in the windfall.

CHAPTER 25

***

Just before dawn Betty Conrad woke to the phone ringing. She scrambled out of bed to answer it.

"Betty, it's Stanley Duncanson. Can I talk to Max?"

"Sure Stanley, one moment," Betty said and met her husband coming down the hall to grab the phone.

When he heard his wife answer the phone, he knew right away that it was Stan Duncanson, the Police Captain for the City of Winona. Max had been up several times during the night, woken by the howling wind. He had stood and watched the storm out his front window at various times and knew he may be called upon to help with locating lost or stranded hunters.

"Yeah Stan," Max said, retrieving the phone from his wife's outstretched hand.

"Max, I was hoping you could help us out. I've been getting phone calls all night long. We must have a couple dozen hunters unaccounted for. Any chance you could go up and take a look?" Chief Duncanson inquired.

"Yeah, I'll get ready and head to my hangar, hopefully I can get my plane off the ground," Max said, looking out the window at the drifts across his driveway and in the streets.

The first thing Max Conrad did was make some phone calls to his flying students and some friends. He would need help with his plane. The wind and deep snow would make getting his plane out of the hangar and off the ground more than a one man job. Max put on some warm clothes and made the treacherous drive to the little Winona airport and his hangar.

When he arrived at his hangar, many of the men volunteering to help him were already there. The last plane into the hangar from his last flight two days ago was his yellow Piper Cub. It was lightweight and would be hard to handle in the high winds, but it would be the easiest plane to get out, the snow piled high against the sides of the hangar.

While Max readied the Piper Cub, some of Max's friends showed up, several with family members stranded somewhere in the Mississippi River bottoms. Everyone was there to help Max get his plane off the ground, a chance to get some encouraging information about their loved ones.

John Bean, one of Max's young students volunteered to go up with Max. As dawn emerged, so did the winds. A brief calm had followed the snow and howling winds. The temperatures plummeted as the front came through. Now, the winds had fired back up and were blowing at 50 knots, making this flight a dangerous one indeed. Max would fly while John helped serve as spotter, looking for the many missing hunters.

Max assessed the situation and was concerned. On any normal day, he never would have attempted to go up in any plane, let alone his lightweight Piper Cub with the wind blowing this hard. The snow and clouds had cleared, leaving blue skies. But, the temperature was now 10 degrees, a far cry from the high of 60 degrees just 24 hours earlier. The high winds and deep snow on the runway would make for a treacherous takeoff, but Max knew he needed to go up and try to pinpoint the location of the hunters.

Police Captain, Stanley Duncanson, had informed him that the diesel tug, Throckmorton was on the main channel, and would dispatch the United States Engineer's launch, Chippewa, to rescue the hunters in the backwaters between the Minnesota bluffs and the main channel of the Mississippi River. Max Conrad's job was to locate hunters and circle the stranded hunters until the Chippewa could pinpoint their location and make their way to them. That is, if the Chippewa and other rescue boats, could make it through the ice, now built up in the backwater sloughs. The freezing temperatures overnight had caused any body of water without much flow to freeze over. Captain C.F. Fuller, aboard the Throckmorton, hoped the hunters could make it to the main channel, where rescue would be easier.

With Max and John in the small plane, Max's students and other men opened the hangar door and pulled the plane out tail first. The men waded into the knee deep snow and pulled the plane out into the brutal wind and cold. All available hands grabbed onto the wings to hold the light plane down or it would have been blown over backwards. Max revved the engine and the men ran alongside, still holding the wings until the wind lifted the plane up. Visibility improved as Max cleared the swirling wind and snow on the ground. Max headed toward the river and its endless miles of backwaters, not sure what he would find.

Right away Max saw that a great challenge in front of him was keeping his little airplane moving against the north wind. Leaving the airport and heading toward the river bottoms took him directly into the biting northern wind. His plane's airspeed indicator pointed to 80, but with the wind coming at him, he figured he was only going 20 to 30 miles per hour. Just after passing a couple sloughs and getting into the heart of the Mississippi River bottoms, he saw a black lab running up and down on the frozen slough that had only a day earlier been open water.

"Look! A dog!" Max shouted over the roar of the engine and the howling wind. "Keep an eye on it and a sign for hunters, I'm going to swing around.

John Bean hung on as the plane turned with the wind and was instantly caught up in the gusts, rocketing past where Max had just seen the dog; his airspeed indicator now reading 130 miles per hour.

"There!" As Max was completing his banking turn, he saw someone standing in the middle of a small marshy area. Once he leveled out, he was able to see what appeared to be a boy, broken through the ice to his waist. The boy waved, but then fell forward, his chest resting on the ice.

He and John were in the air a matter of minutes, and he feared that he had already seen what would be a familiar sight that day.

"Coming around again!" Max shouted and banked the plane back into the wind for another look, nearly stalling the plane as it fought for speed again heading into the gale.

This time Max tried to circle around the boy, low enough to see what or who was with him.

"I can see a boat, mostly frozen in the water, and...God, it looks like a body frozen next to it," John said with a shaky voice.

Then Max could see it too. The body of a hunter was motionless, pressed against a barely visible boat, covered in snow, merely ten feet away from the boy, who was still struggling to move and react to the plane, passing by now against the wind only 50 feet above.

"There's someone else, in amongst the tree line!" John shouted.

Sure enough. Max could him now as he

circled, his plane fighting the wind as it began to angle into the wind, being pushed to the right.

Max wanted to land, yet he knew that even if he was able to put the wheels down on the ice and snow, the plane would blow away or flip over. A wrecked plane would not help anyone today. He turned back to the airport, still shaken.

CHAPTER 26

***

At 6:30 A.M., Tuesday, November 12th, Nic Steffes and his son Buzz were not headed to work at Nic's Garage. Their day would not be filled with repairing automobiles belonging to people in Winona. Today, a foot and a half of snow lay on the ground, with drifts over four feet high created by the powerful winds that blew the snow around until shortly before dawn. Now, the skies were beginning to clear and the winds were roaring again, continuing to blow the snow, creating road blocking drifts, and numbing wind chills.

When word got out that Max Conrad, a local light aircraft pilot was braving the wind and cold temperatures to go up in search of stranded hunters, Nic and Buzz, along with other citizens drove through the snow to the little Winona Airport to lend a hand.

CHAPTER 27

***

"We can't cross here," Bob said, the collar up on his coat in an attempt to shelter his face from the cold wind rapidly increasing in the early morning light. "I'm freezing. Fighting through all the brush in the dark, I'm soaking wet. Let's get that fire started and take a break."

Ed opened the lid to the shell box for what felt like the 100th time since they started walked to the mouth of Twin Lakes in the snow, only hours earlier. The big man sheltered his valuable cargo from the wind instinctively, relieved to still have embers glowing inside. Bob still had his canister of matches, but keeping the fire burning was a great sense of security against the cold, with no guarantee they could get a fire going with damp wood and high winds. Bob was busy nearby kicking away the deep snow to find some ground for an attempt at rekindling a fire. Satisfied that they still had a chance to get a fire going, Ed set the shell box in the snow. Carefully he pointed the open end of the shell box away from the wind, and began gathering small mostly dry sticks from low hanging dead branches. The two men gently removed the glowing sticks and embers from the metal box and, squatting side by side to shelter their fire from the wind, added kindling until they again had a blaze.

"Ahh! That feels good!" Ed said, warming his hands and feet at the same time, stooping over the building flames.

"We can't stay too long," Bob said, "We still need to find a way out of here. We need to find a way to get to the main channel."

"I agree," Ed replied with a nod.

All the tension between the two men had vanished now. The warmth of the fire and a new plan had again given them some hope that they would find a way home. The day was just starting, so taking a moment to warm themselves by a fire was now possible.

Suddenly, their attention left the fire as a small airplane flew by following Pickerel Run.

"A plane!" yelled Bob, jumping up from the fire and running toward the banks of the small slough, looking up to see the little plane flying slowly as it fought the power of the wind, as it began to turn.

Within seconds, even before Ed could join Bob on the shore, the plane had made its turn, and pushed by the wind, came screaming back past them. Bob jumped up and down, waving his arms, gingerly stepping out onto the new ice on Pickerel Run.

"Hey! Hey!" Ed yelled, now standing on the shoreline. "Get back here before you fall through!" He'll see the smoke!"

Bob, realizing that in his excitement he risked breaking through the ice, now came back to the shoreline with Ed and watched as the little yellow plane began to turn again, this time struggling as it tried to turn into the wind.

"I never even heard it until it was practically on top of us!" Bob yelled.

"The wind. The wind is from the north and the plane came out of the south. No wonder we didn't hear it," Ed said. "He saw the smoke though,"

Both men stood and watched the plane make another run along the slough slowly, battling the head wind.

"Looks like two guys on board," Ed said.

As the plane came parallel to them, its air speed alarmingly slowed in the wind barely above the tree tops, the pilot, with window down, repeatedly motioned toward the Wisconsin bluffs and the main channel of the Mississippi.

Both men stood and watched as the plane continued on flying slowly against the wind toward the main channel, then hooking upriver and disappearing.

"Well, it looks as if your second plan is the one we need to go with," Ed said, stooping to pet Duke, wiggling with nervous energy beside him. "That looked like Max Conrad, and he wants us to head toward the main channel."

"That's where we'll go then," Bob said with a smile. "Let's go Duke!"

The men paused for a few more moments to warm themselves some more by the fire, before carefully placing some glowing embers and sticks into the shell box again for their trip back from where they came, and hopefully farther upriver to where they could find a place to cross Pap Slough or where it diverged from the main channel. It was there that they could get along the shoreline of the river, hopefully still unfrozen, and signal for help. It only made sense. The water in the backwater sloughs moved slower and was mostly becoming frozen over, but the main channel of the Mississippi River had a much greater flow, and, especially in this wind, stood a better chance of being open.

"All right, we should start heading up river, " Ed said after getting as warm as possible in ten minutes, and began to kick snow on the fire.

"Wait!" Bob stopped him. "Throw some timber on the fire. Someone else may be wandering around looking for a way out of here like us. They would probably be pretty happy to find a fire when it's this cold."

Ed nodded in agreement and threw some broken trees limbs in the fire to bring up the flames. Then, sliding their gloves back on and pulling their hats down to ward off the cold wind, the men started back, now walking against the wind, along the narrow strip of land. They would at least be able to follow their tracks from earlier when they stumbled and fought their way along in the dark. With the rejuvenated Duke leading the way, the men made good time. In the daylight they could move faster, able to find the easiest route through the small trees, fallen timber, and brush. One thing that slowed them down a bit, as they neared Bob's boat, was the fact that in the spots where the water overran the land from the high waves flooding the woods, ice had formed amongst the trees making for treacherous walking.

Before they knew it, they were back to the boat. Neither man spoke much during their walk, preferring to keep their faces as protected as possible in the bitter winds, now blowing at least 40 miles per hour. Besides, they both were eager to reach their destination, the main channel of the Mississippi River, their route still unknown. But as they neared the overturned boat, the silence was even more noticeable. Ed walked over to check on Bruce's body, putting his hand on the shoulder of his fallen hunting buddy. Bob gave him plenty of space, walking past the boat and to the shoreline of Pap Slough, looking up and down the now mostly frozen waterway, allowing Ed a chance to be alone for a moment with his friend before continuing on.

CHAPTER 28

***

Nic and Buzz arrived at the little Winona Airport just as Max was attempting to land in the powerful winds. A group of men, many of which were Max's students had come out of the warmth of the hangar to watch the landing. Nic and Buzz pulled their hats down tight, turned up the collars on their coats, and hurried to join the men.

Many people, including Nic and Buzz, had brought boxes of supplies such as food, matches, and even whisky with the hope that Max would be able to drop sacks of these supplies to the stranded hunters he spotted as he flew over the backwaters.

The Steffes family had known Max Conrad for years. Max was very familiar with Bob, and Nic hoped Max may have some good news for his family.

The little yellow Piper Cub was coming in very slowly against the wind. As Max brought the plane closer to the ground for a touchdown, gusts of wind pushed it around, causing the wings to dip to the 'gasps' of the men anxiously waiting. The plane drifted as the pilot worked to correct its course, finally setting it down to the applause of the spectators. In no time, the plane slowed, aided by its initial slow speed, high winds, and snow covered runway. The men began running out through the blowing snow and cold to help guide Max and John into the hangar. Nic and Buzz joined in, pushing the plane by its wings through the snow and eventually into the warmth of the hangar.

Once the doors were shut, everyone began to talk at once. "Did they see any hunters?", "Did they spot the rescue boat on the main channel?", and "Were they going to make it back up to drop supplies to stranded hunters?"

Some men immediately began refueling the

plane, not waiting for Max to answer all the questions. They knew he was going back up. Too many hunters were counting on them to help those still out in the marsh.

"Yeah, I'm going back up. As soon as we're refueled and the supplies are loaded, we'll head back out," Max said, climbing down out of his plane and grabbing a cup of coffee.

"Was the Corp. of Engineers boat out on the channel?" someone asked.

"Yeah, it was coming up river, just south of Fountain City. Should be there by now. Looks like it will stick close there and send their smaller boat, the Chippewa, out to pluck hunters off the islands…if the hunters can make it to the main channel," Max continued.

Everyone wanted to know if Max recognized anybody he saw from the plane. He listed off names of guys he may have seen, careful not to get anybody's hopes up, not willing to confirm any identities.

"It was hard to be sure who I was seeing out there," Max continued, in between ordering the group as to how he wanted supplies packaged. "Keep it light! Some food, matches for sure, maybe a small bottle of whiskey wrapped in a towel for cushion, skip anything that's heavy. Tie the sacks tight. They may hit hard when I drop them."

"Max, did you recognize my….." Nic began.

"Plenty of guys out there, so let's hustle up and get me back in the air," Max continued. "I saw some lucky guy managed to get a fire going at the mouth of Twin Lakes. But…. I also saw where a young guy was frozen in the ice, still alive, struggling to get out. His lab was still running around on top of the ice. The kid waved at the plane, but," silence fell over the hangar as Max told them about the gut wrenching scene that played out in from of him earlier, "there wasn't anything I could do."

"We did what we could," John Bean spoke up, reassuring the pilot.

"Max," Nic said, casting a look toward Buzz, "was the dog a black lab?"

"Yes," Max responded, now realizing that the information he was providing the other men, matched Bob and Duke's description.

Nic sighed. "Where did you see the kid stuck in the ice?"

"Pickerel Run," Max said with a grimace, seeing no relief in Nic's face.

As they finished loading the Piper Cub and were helping Max Conrad and John Bean with the takeoff, running alongside, wings in hand to keep the plane from flipping in the wind until Max had enough chance to gain some speed, Nic Steffes couldn't help thinking, "Was his son at the mouth of Twin Lakes sitting by a fire, stuck in the ice, perhaps dead by now somewhere along Pickerel Run, or was he elsewhere, still waiting to be rescued?"

CHAPTER 29

***

As Bob waited at the shoreline of Twin Lakes, giving Ed a moment or two at the boat with Bruce before continuing on upriver, he looked out across the lake, shaking his head at the fact that less than 12 hours earlier, the lake in front of him was wide open. At this time yesterday, it was over 50 degrees with a light wind and no snow. Now, Bob figured they had gotten 15 or 16 inches of snow, and it would surprise him if it was over 10 degrees. The wind chill probably pushed the mercury to well below zero.

Twelve hours ago, Ed was just the enemy – a guy whom he had competed against, fought with, and envied. Now, omitting their brief confrontation at the mouth of the lake, they were dependent upon one another. Ed was working hard to keep an ember glowing in the shell box, access to a fire that they have already needed. The act of creating a shelter last night with the boat, finding firewood to keep them warm, and working on a game plan for a rescue required both the men to come together. The whole 24 hours seemed too illogical to believe. Here they were, stuck in the frozen backwaters of the Mississippi River together, joining forces in an attempt to survive.

"All right, let's go!" Ed said, bringing Bob back to the reality they were in.

Ed tossed Bob a candy bar. "I completely forgot about these," Ed said fighting back some emotions. "Bruce had a stash of candy bars in his coat pocket."

"Thanks," Bob replied, acknowledging the gesture with a small pat on the big man's back.

The men continued on the strip of land, beginning to become broken up now by wider sections of woods, circling around bays as they came to the upper end of Twin Lakes. They talked as they went now, keeping it to school related topics. Was Ed happy to have graduated? Who was their favorite high school teacher? Would the Minnesota Gopher football team finish the season with the #1 ranking?

The woods widened considerable once they reached the end of Twin Lakes.

"We could head toward the Minnesota bluffs," Ed suggested, almost questioningly.

"Yeah, but we'd still have to cross Dark Slough to get to the highway just north of Minnesota City," Bob replied. "That's usually a pretty strong flow. The ice may not be strong enough for us to cross. Besides, that's quite a hike, with a lot of frozen potholes to cross between here and Highway 61.

Ed nodded his head in agreement, rubbing his cold, whiskered face, "You're right. Let's keep headin' up river along Pap Slough. I'm fairly certain we'll hit the main channel where it leaves the big water."

A decision was made. They continued walking. Pap Slough was to their right, a frozen channel now about 75 yards wide.

The extent of the night's high winds was evident as their terrain became more hardwoods than the small saplings of the narrow strips of woods that were more marsh than forest. Bigger trees such as elm and birch were down, uprooted by the heavy snow and winds. Duke, who earlier had no problem walking amongst the small trees and brush of the marshy lowlands, now slowed down as he, like his owner and new companion, had to negotiate the deeper snow and downed trees.

"I wonder if my dad and brother are trying to find me?" Bob asked, turning toward Ed so his voice could be heard in the wind.

"Not sure what they could do," Ed replied.

"I guess," Bob continued. "I suppose they could try taking a boat out into the main channel and come in that way to look for me."

"Did your dad know where you were headed when you went out?" Ed questioned.

"Yeah, he knows where I always go," Bob said, slowing as he walked so they didn't have to battle the wind as they talked.

"I don't think too many guys are crazy enough to mess with the main channel today," Ed said, realizing that he wasn't making his travel companion feel any better. "I mean…they could try coming across from Fountain City, but with these winds, the river would be pretty treacherous."

"Probably, but I could see him giving it a shot," Bob said, hopefully.

"Yeah, he's a tough old bird," Ed replied. "He's probably making his way through the woods right now, coming to look for you. My dad too. Marie is worried I bet," Ed said, instantly knowing he brought up a sore subject.

An uncomfortable silence took over for a moment. Bob nodded, but kept walking, looking straight ahead.

"She seems pretty nice," Bob finally said matter of factly.

"Yeah, she is," Ed said, wondering where the conversation was heading.

"I wouldn't mind finding a girlfriend as nice as her someday," Bob said, shaking his head as if thinking aloud.

"Well, maybe Marie can find a friend for you," Ed said, smiling.

Bob smirked, "Sure. Why not!" he said with a laugh.

Just then, a roar of an airplane could be heard in the wind. Both men stopped walking, Bob grabbed Duke to halt the dog's movements. Bob and Ed stood listening, uncertain which direction the sound was coming from.

"The slough!" Bob said and ran through the woods, hurdling logs as he ran the short distance to the shoreline of Pap Slough, just in time to see the little yellow Piper Cub fly by, following the slough heading south.

CHAPTER 30

***

Max Conrad was determined to keep going up in his plane all day if necessary to locate and assist hunters trapped in the river bottoms. The previous day's balmy weather had caught everyone off guard. Those who were stuck in the maze of sloughs and backwaters today were facing below zero wind chills and over a foot of snow. Their routes to the boat landings or main channels had been frozen over. Those who made it through the night, even lightly dressed as they all probably were, would certainly benefit from Max and John dropping supplies such as matches and food.

Max was hoping his discussion about the boy in the ice did not disturb Nic Steffes. Max had done business at Nic's garage for years. He was a good man. He also knew Nic's son, Bob, and hoped that the hunter he saw in dire straits along Pickerel Run was not his son. He knew Bob to be a hard-working, athletic young man. Bob's death would be devastating to the Steffes family.

Max's second flight of the day would take him up river along Dark Slough, farther from the main channel and closer to the Minnesota bluffs. His plan was to follow the slough for about five miles, then turn east toward the main channel of the Mississippi River, pinpoint the location of the Throckmorton, then circle back to the airport. The first five miles would be against the wind, and he would be burning a lot of fuel. He figured his slowed air speed going against the wind would make it easier for John and himself to spot stranded hunters. Circling around the hunters, making a second slow pass against the wind, would allow a more accurate drop.

Dark Slough had a little more flow, running parallel to the bluffs, not too far from Highway 61, but before he made the five mile run, they had circled four times helping hunters, with John making supply drops in the trees, avoiding drops on the iced up slough.

His turn to the east made for difficult flying. The strong north wind kept trying to push his plane off course. The woods below him were thick, with a few sporadic partially ice covered potholes, filled with ducks fleeing the storm just a day earlier. It wasn't until he spotted the diesel tug, Throckmorton, positioned just upriver from Fountain City, Wisconsin, that he began his flight back down river toward the airport. The tug was moored, and even with his great size, it was twisting and bouncing on the high waves of the river. Men on the tug were standing in its bridge, watching Max's flight. Each time he circled to drop supplies they would know the relative location of the stranded hunters. Max needed to fly high enough to be seen by the Throckmorton, but low enough to spot hunters. He was constantly adjusting his altitude while fighting the wind.

As he was making his turn to head down river along Pap Slough, John yelled, "Hunters! Max, pretty sure I saw hunters running through the woods back there. Come around!"

"Where!?" Max shouted over the roar of the engine and howling wind around his aircraft.

"West shoreline! Two guys and a dog!" John shouted back, shifting in his seat to get a visual on the hunters, at the same time, grabbing a bag for a supply drop.

Max began banking the plane back toward the Minnesota bluffs and back upriver, his plane bucking the wind as he again swung into the headwind. Seeing the hunters on his return trip to the airport meant that he would have the wind at his back and his airspeed would be greatly increased, making drops much more difficult. His initial plan was to make the drop coming into the wind, but the wind pushed his plane off course, and unless he wanted to make another 360 degree turn, he would have to make the drop in a tailwind.

"Gotta make this one quick, John!" Max shouted. "The winds got me off course already!"

The Piper Cub sailed along Pap Slough swiftly in the wind. John opened the door and hesitated a moment, the plane too far from the shoreline for an accurate drop.

"Let it go!" Max shouted.

The bag hit close to the shoreline and Max continued down river, hoping to fly past Twin Lakes, then on toward Mallard Lake and across Prairie Island to the airport.

CHAPTER 31

***

Instinctively, Duke ran past the men and out onto the ice. When the Piper Cub dropped the sack, it had been caught in the wind and sailed clear of the woods and landed on the frozen slough, finally skidding to a stop in the middle of the 75 yard wide waterway.

"Fetch it up Duke!" Bob yelled.

The young lab bounded out onto the ice in pursuit of the gunny sack. The dog was nearly there when the ice gave way underneath him, and he slipped into the icy water.

"Duke!" Bob yelled and took a couple steps

onto the ice, only to be held back from behind by Ed.

"Give him a second to climb out!" Ed yelled as the wind blew strongly along the shoreline of Pap Slough, pushing snow into their faces.

Duke floundered, bringing all four legs into the water in an attempt to swim, but quickly brought his front legs onto the ice, trying to pull himself out. As soon as he went vertical in the water, just as he had the day before in the high waves of Twin Lakes, his head went under water. When he went under, his front legs went under with him and his head bobbed up again, snow falling into the water onto the head of the confused dog from the edge of the hole. This sequence continued; a furious confusion as the dog battled his instinct to swim, only to realize that there was no space, just a ring of ice around him. Then, front legs went onto the ice again.

Bob pulled free from Ed's grip and, after walking out onto the ice 20 yards, dropped to his hands and knees in the deep snow and began crawling toward his dog, panicking in the cold water for the second time in two days.

Ed knew he wasn't going to stop the 16 year old from making an attempt to free his dog from the water. Bob slithered closer, his feet pushing him forward in the deep snow. As he neared Duke, Bob stretched his arm out attempting to grab his collar. Duke saw his owner coming to his rescue and turned to exit the ice on the edge closest to Bob. The combined weight of Bob and his young black lab on the same patch of thin ice was too much. The ice gave way under Bob and he slid in the loose snow headfirst into the water, joining Duke in the icy water. As Bob slid, he pushed Duke from his hold on the ice and both disappeared under the surface of the water momentarily.

Ed swore through the wind, taking a few steps in the direction of Bob, grabbed onto the ice, only to have more deep snow tumble into his face and more ice breaking off the ever increasing hole.

Bob finally caught hold of a solid hand hold with one hand and, reaching around, put Duke in a headlock, trying to shove his dog onto the ice.

"Hang on! I'm grabbing a branch! " shouted Ed, and he ran, stumbling as he went, into the woods and frantically began pulling on any fallen tree or branch he could find.

CHAPTER 32

***

"Max! Turn around!" yelled John Bean, looking back and seeing a dog, then a man crashed through the ice seeking to retrieve the bag he had just dropped on the snow and ice of Pap Slough.

"What!?" Max yelled back in the noisy cockpit of his Piper Cub.

"I saw a black dog run out onto the ice just after the gunny sack hit. The dog went through the ice, then a guy went in after him," John rattled off to his pilot.

Without responding, Max Conrad banked his

plane back into the wind and veered parallel with Pap Slough, with the Throckmorton and Chippewa to his right, just on the other side of a narrow island separating Pap Slough and the choppy open water of the Mississippi River. Max instantly saw the dark shapes in the water, surrounded by the snow covered slough. The diesel tug probably wasn't any more than a quarter mile from where the man and dog were now battling to pull themselves onto the ice.

"There they are!" John shouted. "There's another guy on shore, see him?"

"Yeah!" Max said, his plane slowed as he flew directly into the wind.

Both men in the plane, going no more than 25 miles per hour in the head wind, flew directly over the narrow island and Max could clearly see as he passed, the face of Bob Steffes, attempting to lift his dog free of the icy water.

Max then took a right and headed toward the Throckmorton. There wasn't anything he could do for young Bob just then, but if he could get the Chippewa to the island, they would be very near Bob and the desperate situation.

Max fought the crosswind and headed out over the main channel directly toward the Throckmorton and the Chippewa, just pulling away from the tug and heading downriver.

"I'm going to bring the plane right over the Chippewa into the wind, wave them up river!" yelled Max and he again brought his plane into the wind, his speed slowed.

John Bean opened the door of the cockpit in the strong wind and with exaggerated arm motions, urged the Chippewa to turn toward the little island with the two men and dog just on the other side.

"Are they turning?!" Max yelled as he passed the Chippewa.

"Yeah! They're coming about!" John shouted back.

Max made three consecutive passes over the spot where Bob and Duke battled to hang on; the Chippewa battled the waves of the main channel, drawing near the island.

CHAPTER 33

***

Ed dropped the smoking shell box and used all his might to break off the upper end of a downed tree. He was now dragging it out onto the slough where Bob was struggling to hang onto the ice and lift his dog out. Max Conrad had just flown past and could be seen still, flying over the main channel just on the other side of the little island across the slough they were on.

"Ed! Don't come over to this side! Go around!" Bob screamed.

Ed followed Bob's urgent instructions and began making his way around the opposite side of the hole, only to feel the ice giving way underneath him. He lunged forward, pulling the tree branch with him, and flopped down onto the snow, narrowly escaping going in himself. He wasn't out of trouble yet. Water crept up through the snow underneath the big man as he scrambled forward in the snow, ice giving way underneath him. Ed tried to roll clear of the water the best he could in the deep snow as water enveloped his legs.

Reaching out with the branch, Ed yelled, "Grab on! I'll try to pull you out!"

Bob grabbed hold. With something solid to hang onto to keep him from going under, Bob reached under Duke, and with one big shove, pushed the dog onto the snow covered ice. Duke stumbled, trying to get his frozen feet under him, and moved clear of the hole.

"Ahh!" Ed yelled, straining to kick himself free of the half submerged slab of ice, and pull Bob free at the same time.

With what was left of Bob's energy, he kicked in the water and pulled his upper body onto the ice. Using his arms, he pulled his way through the snow, with Ed using his legs to drive them both through the snow and slush toward the opposite shoreline.

Feeling solid ice once again under them, Ed

said, out of breath, "I think we're good. Can you get up?"

Bob lay in the snow, completely drained of energy from the cold and the struggle to keep he and Duke from going under.

"Bob! Can you make it the rest of the way to shore?!" Ed yelled, willing Bob to make it the remaining 15 yards to solid ground.

"Give me a hand," Bob was able to say at last.

Ed reached down and helped Bob to his feet and both men, soaking wet stumbled through the snow and wind the rest of the way to the shore and the sandy, wooded island.

Once they hit the shoreline, Bob collapsed, his clothes dripping, but beginning to freeze solid.

"Matches? I'll get a fire going," Ed said, patting Bob's clothing, searching for the little canister of matches he carried.

Feeling the canister, Ed dug in Bob's pocket, pulled it out and charged just inside the wood line and began pulling whatever sticks and cattails he could find free of the snow.

Bob watched, too cold to speak, as the big man ripped bark free of a downed tree and began using his own knife to scrape away some tinder from underneath.

"You learned that from me," mumbled Bob,

still on the ground, fending off Duke, who was wet and concerned, trying to sniff his face.

"Damn right!" Ed said with a chuckle, kicking away snow next to Bob, beginning to clear a spot for a fire.

"Where's the shell box?" Bob asked, still lying in the snow, but trying to look around.

"Well, I couldn't save your butt and haul around that shell box at the same time, now could I?!" Ed said, snapping sticks, preparing to make a fire.

"I suppose not," Bob said, shivering uncontrollably.

With a small pile of frozen sticks in place, Ed stuck some of the shavings from underneath the bark below the sticks. Ed shuffled into place, his back to the wind and carefully pulled out a match.

"Wish me luck, I may only get one shot at this," Ed said, striking the match, watching it flare briefly then lowering it under the sticks and blowing slightly, watched as a flame took hold.

"Not bad," Bob said and began easing through the snow closer.

"Yeah, not bad huh! And you got to use gas!" Ed said laughing.

"No bragging!" Bob said laughing with relief as the flames continued to increase, Ed feeding more sticks.

"Let's get some of those wet clothes off you," Ed said as he helped Bob into a sitting position and began peeling off his wet coat and flooded hip boots. "But I'm not rubbing your feet!"

Both men laughed as Max Conrad flew over again.

"The main channel is just on the other side of this island," Ed said. "I'm going to take a look," and he disappeared over a little rise on the island.

Less than a minute later Ed returned. "I have good news and bad news," Ed said with a smile.

"Good news first," Bob said, now sitting close to the growing fire with Duke, rubbing his hands, trying to get some feeling back.

" A boat is about to come ashore just over that little rise," Ed said laughing.

"Bad news?" Bob inquired.

"You're going to live to see my team beat you next near in baseball!" Ed said with a haughty laugh. "If I get a chance to bat in the ninth, that is."

Both men laughed hard, Ed standing, slapping Bob on the back.

"You know, I never doubted you'd pull through, you're one tough runt!" Ed said, still laughing.

"Well, I guess we're even," Bob said. "Thanks!"

Shouts could be heard through the woods and men suddenly appeared, coming toward the hunters, competitors, and friends.

EPILOGUE

***

The Armistice Day storm of 1940 was a tragic event in the Midwest. Nobody was able to predict that a day where temperatures would reach nearly 60 degrees could change so fast, with two feet of snow and temperatures dropping below zero in a 24 hour period. Many record low pressure readings were set during the storm.

Most people were caught off guard. Nearly half of the 49 people who died in Minnesota were hunters. Duck hunters along the Mississippi River valley perished as they succumbed to the cold, stranded out in the marshes and river bottoms, often with only light weight clothing to protect them. Waterfowl hunters reported seeing thousands of ducks ahead of the cold front. They could have easily have shot their limits if they were not busy trying to escape the storm or seeking shelter on the many islands in the river bottoms.

This book is a tribute to those who lost their lives.

The idea for writing this book came on the ten year anniversary of my father's death. My father, Bob Steffes, was 52 years old when I was born. He, as well as my grandfather, Nic, whom I never met were avid outdoorsmen. I have tried to follow in their footsteps with my love for fishing and hunting. I try to share this love for outdoor adventure with my son Cal, age 12, who is on the cover of my first book, Dirty Hands. My father had a stroke that disabled him when I was only nine years old. Yet that didn't stop him from driving me down to the river so I could go fishing while he sat in his station wagon or in a lawn chair along the bank. I always knew if I had behaved myself as a kid when I would ask my dad to take me fishing or hunting every Sunday. If he said "no", I knew I must have screwed up sometime during the week. Hunting and fishing was a carrot he dangled for me, much like I do with my own son.

My father ended up working for Douglas Aircraft in California, served in the U.S. Navy from 1942 to 1944, then coming back to Winona to become a mail carrier. I never was able to go duck hunting with him due to his stroke, but was able to tag along with the guys in our deer hunting group. He was able to use a .357 pistol for deer, since his left arm was no longer useful. I know he missed duck hunting after his stroke. Duke was really his favorite hunting dog.

My father passed away in 2001. My mother followed in 2004. They were wonderful parents and I miss them greatly every day.

When my dad was sitting at home in Winona, and I was living in La Crescent, just down river, my mom would often call me and tell me to drive to Winona and take my dad out for a beer at the Elks Club. It was here that he would tell me, while sipping on a Pabst Blue Ribbon and munching peanuts, stories about trapping, hunting, and about his time in the navy. It was during these times that I learned about his adventure, hunting during the Armistice Day Storm.

I had to take some literary privilege in a few areas. My father was really 23 years old and hunting alone during the storm. His motor had frozen up and he had in fact rowed the boat in, battling high waves to make it to the boat landing after dark. His nemesis was really Earl Kreutzer, not Ed, and they battled it out on a fast pitch softball field, Graham and McGuires against Swedes Bar. Their relationship was positive throughout. Swede, the owner of Swedes Bar is in fact, the father of my brother-in-law. Swede Gordon was a wonderful guy and is truly missed. Many of the names I used during the baseball games came from the box scores of my father's fast pitch softball games. My dad loved playing softball and always spoke highly of his teammates.

Sonny Ehlers was really my neighbor growing up. He was a tremendous guy who loved the river and duck hunting. He and Norman Roloff were hunting north of Winona in the Reads Landing area during the storm. They were some of the lucky ones, surviving their ordeal. Sonny Ehlers and his family were great neighbors and friends. Growing up, I would wait for Sonny to come home from duck hunting. Sonny would give me the curly tail feathers of the drake mallards he shot. Sonny died last year and will be greatly missed.

I tried to be as historically accurate as possible when writing about the city of Winona and the events of the Armistice Day Storm. Liberace really did play at St. Teresa's College, now part of the Winona State University campus, the night of the storm. The sloughs and waterways mentioned in the story are places I have hunted and fished with friends and family.

Max Conrad was a real hero. The Winona Airport is now named after him. He and his student, John Bean, were instrumental in the rescue attempts made with the help of the government boats Throckmorton and Chippewa. Both men were nominated for the Carnegie Medal for their heroism. Thank you Mr. Conrad and Mr. Bean for risking your life to save others.

Lastly, thank you to my family for again allowing me to pursue my writing.

ABOUT THE AUTHOR

Jon Steffes is an elementary teacher in La Crescent, Minnesota. His desire to create books that would interest young people, specifically those who are interested in the outdoors has led him to this book. His first book, Dirty Hands, was published just four months previous to this one. More books will be coming soon, all focused on the outdoors and taking place in the Mississippi River valley that Jon loves so much.

Jon enjoys teaching, spending summers running the recreation program for the City of La Crescent, and of course, hunting and fishing. Jon and his wife, JoAnn, have one son, Cal, and two daughters, Kathryn and Meghan.

Made in the USA
Monee, IL
01 December 2019

17730454R00108